What people are saying about ...

# KYLE IDLEMAN

"Kyle knows where we live and where we could live with God's help. He is committed to helping us move in the right direction. If you need a helping hand in your journey, he'll point you to the right Person."

**Max Lucado,** pastor of Oak Hills
Church and author of *Grace*

"A wise, mature person is known for his understanding. The more pleasant his words, the more persuasive he is. Kyle Idleman is one of today's great young teachers. He's a brilliant, compassionate, and thoughtful communicator who presents the truth of Scripture in a fresh, relevant, and persuasive way."

**Rick Warren,** author of *The
Purpose Driven Life*

"Kyle will challenge you to grow from a fair-weather fan to a full-time follower of Christ."

**Craig Groeschel,** senior pastor of
LifeChurch.tv and author of *Fight*

"Kyle will challenge even the most obedient Christians to relook at their relationship with Christ."

**Mike Huckabee,** former governor of Arkansas and bestselling author

"Like his preaching, Kyle's writings will bring you face-to-face with areas you need to change and the One who has the power to change you."

**Dave Stone,** senior pastor of Southeast Christian Church and author of *Raising Your Kids to Love the Lord*

"Fresh, insightful, practical—Kyle's writing and teaching are helping countless people. I'm thrilled with how God is using him to challenge and encourage both Christians and those who are checking out the faith. Count me among his many fans!"

**Lee Strobel,** bestselling author and professor at Houston Baptist University

"Kyle cuts through all the nonsense and takes us straight to what is most important spiritually."

**Jud Wilhite,** senior pastor of Central Christian Church and author of *The God of Yes*

"Kyle is a great communicator, always driving home his messages in powerful, compelling, and practical ways."

**David Novak,** CEO of YUM! Brands
(Taco Bell, Pizza Hut, KFC) and
author of *Taking People with You*

# 40 DAYS

## TO LASTING CHANGE

# 40 DAYS
## TO LASTING CHANGE

AN **AHA** CHALLENGE

## kyle idleman

David C Cook®
*transforming lives together*

40 DAYS TO LASTING CHANGE
Published by David C Cook
4050 Lee Vance View
Colorado Springs, CO 80918 U.S.A.

David C Cook Distribution Canada
55 Woodslee Avenue, Paris, Ontario, Canada N3L 3E5

David C Cook U.K., Kingsway Communications
Eastbourne, East Sussex BN23 6NT, England

The graphic circle C logo is a registered trademark of David C Cook.

LCCN 2014948794
ISBN 978-0-7814-1268-1
eISBN 978-1-4347-0900-4

© 2015 Kyle Idleman
Published in association with the literary agency of The
Gates Group, www.the-gates-group.com.

The Team: Alex Field, Amy Konyndyk, Helen Macdonald, Karen Athen
Cover Design: Nick Lee
Cover Photo: Shutterstock

Printed in the United States of America
First Edition 2015

1 2 3 4 5 6 7 8 9 10

101714

# CONTENTS

# INTRODUCTION

## *Selfless Help*

If you're looking for a self-help book, you can put this one down. Bookstores and libraries are filled with them—including some hilarious titles and topics—but this is not one.

AHA is not a self-help process. It's an "I can't help myself" process.

The goal of *40 Days to Lasting Change: An AHA Challenge* is not to find ways to change ourselves—it's to seek and encounter God in ways that allow Him to change us. Instead of self-help, we are asking for God's help. We are declaring that we are helpless. We are inviting God to do what we can't do on our own.

AHA is a spiritual experience that brings about supernatural change. More specifically, AHA is "a sudden recognition that leads to an honest moment that brings lasting change." With striking consistency, AHA always has three ingredients:

1. A Sudden Awakening
2. Brutal Honesty
3. Immediate Action

If any one of these ingredients is missing, it short-circuits the transformation process

If there is an awakening and honesty, but no action, then AHA doesn't happen.

If there is awakening and action, but honesty is overlooked, AHA will be short-lived.

But when God's Word and the Holy Spirit bring these three things together in your life, you will experience AHA—a God-given moment that changes everything.

## Your AHA Journey

This book is about humbly seeking God and opening your heart to His Word and His Spirit. It's about making yourself available to discover how God wants to use Awakening, Honesty, and Action to bring about growth and spiritual transformation in your life. It's about living in the Father's house. It's about interacting with God, walking and talking with Him, and learning to recognize His voice and His ways in our lives. It's about our lifelong journey of awakening to His guidance, living openly and honestly before Him, and taking action as He guides us. And it's about our transformation, initial and ongoing, as our Father shapes us into the image of His Son through His extravagant love and grace.

Our forty-day journey together centers on the parable of the prodigal son. It's my favorite AHA story. With this one short parable, Jesus revealed so much about our heavenly Father. It's almost impossible to read this story without finding yourself in it. My prayer is that it will be impossible not to find yourself and encounter God in a transformative way. Let's begin your story with the story Jesus told in Luke 15:11–32:

> There was a man who had two sons. The younger one said to his father, "Father, give me my share of the estate." So he divided his property between them.
>
> Not long after that, the younger son got together all he had, set off for a distant country and there squandered his wealth in wild living. After he had spent everything, there was a severe famine in that whole country, and he began to be in need. So he went and hired himself out to a citizen of that country, who sent him to his fields to feed pigs. He longed to fill his stomach with the pods that

the pigs were eating, but no one gave him anything.

When he came to his senses, he said, "How many of my father's hired servants have food to spare, and here I am starving to death! I will set out and go back to my father and say to him: Father, I have sinned against heaven and against you. I am no longer worthy to be called your son; make me like one of your hired servants." So he got up and went to his father.

But while he was still a long way off, his father saw him and was filled with compassion for him; he ran to his son, threw his arms around him and kissed him.

The son said to him, "Father, I have sinned against heaven and against you. I am no longer worthy to be called your son."

But the father said to his servants, "Quick! Bring the best robe and put it on him. Put a ring on his finger and sandals on his feet. Bring the fattened calf and kill it. Let's have a feast and celebrate. For this son of mine was dead and is alive again; he was lost and is found." So they began to celebrate.

Meanwhile, the older son was in the field. When he came near the house, he heard music and dancing. So he called one of the servants and asked him what was going on. "Your brother has come," he replied, "and your father has killed the fattened calf because he has him back safe and sound."

The older brother became angry and refused to go in. So his father went out and pleaded with him. But he answered his father, "Look! All these years I've been slaving for you and never disobeyed your orders. Yet you never gave me even a young goat so I could celebrate with my friends. But when this son of yours who has squandered your property with prostitutes comes home, you kill the fattened calf for him!"

"My son," the father said, "you are always with me, and everything I have is yours. But we had to celebrate and be glad, because this

brother of yours was dead and is alive again;
he was lost and is found."

# DAY 1

## Seeking AHA

*Open my eyes that I may see wonderful things in your law.*
Psalm 119:18

*I love witnessing AHA.* I see it almost every weekend at the church where I serve. I listen to people as they tell about the spiritual awakening they have experienced. In that moment there was a beautiful collision. At just the right time, a person's life collides with God's Word and the power of the Holy Spirit, and everything changes.

When Jesus taught about this spiritual transformation, He would most often tell stories. AHA can't fully be explained. There is a sense in which it has to be experienced to be understood. So it's through stories that AHA is best captured. Thankfully, as a pastor, I get to hear a lot of them, especially after writing the book *AHA*. Here are a few that people have shared with me.

Celina wrote,

> After seven years of infertility and my final
> round of fertility drugs in 1996, I stopped
> by the prayer room at Southeast Christian
> Church. As I prayed I asked God to take
> away my desire to become a mother if He
> did not want me to become pregnant. It was
> at that moment I sensed God speak to my
> heart, *You don't need to become pregnant to be a*
> *mother, Celina.* AHA. Two weeks later, Aaron
> and I were chosen by a teenage mother to
> adopt her beautiful baby girl. We welcomed
> our daughter Hannah home four weeks later.
> God is so faithful!

Courtney told me how she turned to compulsive eating to
cope with life. Stress at work, at home, in relationships meant
more desserts and bingeing. Despite trying every self-help
diet and exercise fad, she reached 325 pounds. This seemingly
unstoppable weight gain put her at a point of dark depression,
which only worsened her eating. Finally Courtney realized
something: food was never going to fill the emptiness in her

heart. At church she heard a message from John 6 in which Jesus described Himself as the "Bread of Life." She suddenly realized that she had been trying to make food do for her what only Jesus could do. That was four years and 170 pounds ago. But the outward change was really just a by-product of the inner transformation she experienced when she started looking to Jesus to fill the emptiness of her heart.

AHA.

Ashley's husband was not a Christian. Jim had no interest in church; he didn't think it had anything to offer him. Ashley hoped and prayed he would change his mind and heart. As the years passed, the couple had children. Eventually the children became Christians, and mother and kids prayed that God would open Daddy's heart. But the children grew, and Daddy didn't budge. Ashley wondered why God wasn't answering their prayers. Then after twenty-two years of marriage, she began to see a change in her husband's heart. It was amazing to watch as Jim read his Bible and hungered to learn about God. Then Ashley and her two teens held hands and watched with tears in their eyes as Jim was baptized. What a powerful testimony to two teenagers to witness the answered prayers in the heart of their dad. "All those years I thought God was moving too slow," Ashley said. "God's timing—not mine."

AHA.

Maybe you've prayed for someone and kept praying and kept praying and thought, *What's the point? Nothing's going to change*. And then God breaks through.

Michael wrote, "My big AHA happened when God showed me my obsession with myself. 'Christian' was more of a title than a lifestyle for me, but God has been helping me take the focus off me and put it on Him, where it belongs."

This is the kind of AHA many of us need to experience. We need to be reminded and understand that we are not the center of our faith; we are not the main character in the Bible; church doesn't primarily exist for us; all of this life is for God's glory and God's kingdom and His purposes. This is the AHA of realizing that the focus of the parable of the prodigal son is really on the Father, that the key to "Jesus loves me" is really Jesus.

Kevin's life had been an ongoing struggle with alcoholism. The numerous self-help programs helped for a season, but he was never really on the wagon long enough to fall off. Even when Kevin thought he'd finally hit rock bottom, he managed to fall even further. One day he was listening to a sermon about the Bible passage where Paul said, "Do not get drunk on wine … Instead, be filled with the Spirit" (Eph. 5:18). Immediately, this truth from God's Word opened Kevin's eyes.

He had been looking to alcohol to do for him what the Holy Spirit was meant to do: give him comfort, security, boldness, courage, strength, direction, and hope.

AHA.

# Open Our Eyes

What is God trying to tell you?

I don't think it's an accident that you've picked up this book and come across the AHA message. God wants to speak to us. He is trying to get our attention and wake us up so we can have AHA.

We need an awakening. We need honesty. We need action. And we can begin with seeking and praying for AHA. AHA is an ongoing process of recognizing, returning, and relating to our heavenly Father.

Living the AHA journey is living in expectation.

## My AHA

Pray the AHA prayer of David from Psalm 119:18. Memorize it. Write it down.

_____

_____

_____

_____

Pray it regularly as you read and work through this book. The Message says it well: "Open my eyes so I can see what you show me of your miracle-wonders."

# DAY 2

## *Where Are You?*

*But the LORD God called to the man, "Where are you?"*
Genesis 3:9

Have you ever been lost or disoriented in a mall or maybe an amusement park? You may have known where you were trying to go, but unless you knew where you were starting from, it was impossible to figure out how to get there. When you walked up to the giant map, the first thing you looked for was not your future destination but your current location. Your eyes scanned the map looking for that familiar "You Are Here" symbol.

AHA begins with recognizing your current location. In one area or another, all of us are in the Distant Country. The Distant Country can be defined as any area of our lives where we have walked away from God. It may be that every part of you is living in the Distant Country, or it may just be a specific area of your life where you've left out God. You've posted No Trespassing signs around the perimeter and made it clear that God is not welcome.

How we ended up where we are isn't always clear. There are many reasons why we leave the Father for the Distant Country, but the Bible says that all of us will find ourselves there at some point. Isaiah 59 explains that sin is what separates us from God. And Romans 3 tells us that all of us have sinned. Sin is the vehicle that every one of us has taken to the Distant Country.

In fact, sin—in whatever form we choose it—is universal and has been since the beginning. Way back in the beginning, Adam and Eve found themselves in the Distant Country. You know the story, but here's an abbreviated overview:

> **God:** You can eat anything in the garden except the fruit on that one tree.

> **Serpent:** Did God really say that? What He really meant was you'd know everything. Mmmm, look at this yummy, delicious, juicy fruit.

**Eve:** Soooo shiny—I want it!

**Adam:** Sure, babe, I'll take a bite.

**A & E:** Ah! We're naked!

**Adam:** Come on! I know where we can hide!

It wasn't that Adam and Eve decided to set out for the Distant Country. It was one decision. One line crossed. One turn away from God's directions, and the couple was running and hiding out in the Distant Country, overcome with shame, trying to avoid God.

They were in the Distant Country, and the big, red "You Are Here" arrow showed up in the garden of Eden.

# Only the Beginning

We don't usually think of Adam and Eve's story as a happy one. It's certainly marked with serious loss, regret, and pain. But don't miss the beauty and hope too. You see, Adam and Eve's sin wasn't the end of the story. Neither was their attempt to escape to the Distant Country—or even the dire consequences that they had to face. Those were only the beginning—for Adam and Eve and for all the rest of us. Their fall, and our fall, was the "You Are Here" that was the starting point of their journey.

God didn't abandon Adam and Eve. The most beautiful moment in their story is represented by a short, three-word question: "Where are you?" It can be easy to overlook, but it says everything.

God didn't say, "I know what you did, so you can forget seeing Me again" or "That's it! Forget it. It's all over for you two and the rest of humanity."

Instead, God said, "Where are you?" God came looking for Adam and Eve. He knew they'd headed into the Distant Country to try to avoid Him. He knew that everything had changed. He knew that His Creation had been broken.

But God came after Adam and Eve. It was the beginning of God coming after you and me and every person who would ever exist on this earth. It was the beginning of His redemption story. It was the beginning of His repair. It was the go point of the plan that would cost His Son's life to restore us. But still He came seeking Adam and Eve and us. God extended love across the chasm of guilt and shame that surrounded the Distant Country. And He never stopped.

"Where are you?" God still asks us today. It's a rhetorical question from Him. But it's an invitation filled with longing. It's a plea filled with all the love and expectation and acceptance of the Prodigal Son's Father. It's an open invitation to return home.

It's the beginning of our AHA, the awakening that will point us back home.

## My AHA

I am here.

Pause and identify areas of your life that could be described as Distant Country. Take a moment and give a specific location for this general description. Write down the areas of your life where God is not welcome. If you're feeling artistically inclined, draw the "No Trespassing" signs you have posted for God around your "You Are Here" marker.

_____

_____

_____

_____

_____

_____

List your Distant Country here:

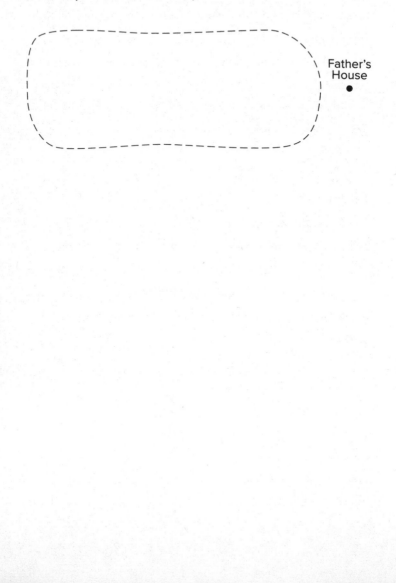

Father's
House

# DAY 3

## *A Tale of Two Fathers*

*A father to the fatherless, a defender of widows,*
*is God in his holy dwelling. God sets the lonely in*
*families, he leads out the prisoners with singing.*

Psalm 68:5–6

A few years ago I came home from work to find that my wife and kids had agreed to dog-sit for some friends. The dog's name was Pork Chop. Everyone was excited about our new houseguest, but when I walked into the room, Pork Chop was not glad to see me. He responded to my presence by peeing on the floor and running into the next room. I tried not to take it too personally, but every time I walked in, I got the same response from Pork Chop.

We later found out that Pork Chop's owners had rescued him from an abusive situation where he'd learned to be afraid

31

of men. He had no reason to fear me—I had taken this dog into my home and provided food and shelter for him—but because he had learned to be afraid of men, he would always run away. I could never get close to him.

That's how some people relate to God.[†] They run away to the Distant Country and never give Him a chance because they've been conditioned to be afraid of Him. They're running from a god that doesn't exist, but their perceptions of God don't line up with the reality of who He is.

## Clouded Vision

Maybe you view God as an **Unreasonable Father** with a long list of rules that seem designed to take all the fun out of life. I've heard God described as "The Great Cosmic Killjoy" whose boundaries are a fence that imprisons rather than a guardrail that protects.

Some people see God as an **Unmerciful Father,** angry and borderline abusive and happily distributing punishment. He's always watching and waiting for you to slip up, and when He catches you, it won't matter how sorry you are—there will be hell to pay—*literally.*

---

†    Minus the peeing.

Unfortunately, religion uses guilt and shame to reinforce rules and present God as an **Unpleasable Father.** That's one of the reasons Jesus wasn't a fan of religion. Maybe you grew up feeling as though your best was never good enough for God. You brought home a B on your report card, but it should have been an A. If you scored fifteen points in the basketball game, you should've scored twenty. Maybe you grew up in a church that perpetuated these beliefs and the view that God never seemed pleased, no matter how much effort you made.

Some people see God as an **Uncaring Father** who wasn't there for them when they needed Him most. Their relationship with God can be summed up like this: "If He doesn't care about me, then I don't care about Him."

Maybe you've adopted this view of God because your earthly father was distant or absent. Maybe you can relate to this letter from a third-grade girl:

*Dear Daddy,*

*I love you so much. When are you going to come see me again? I miss you very much. I love when you take me to the pool. When am I going to spend the night at your house? Have you ever seen my house before? I want to see what your house looks like. When am I going to get to see you again? I love you, Daddy.*

# Our Real Heavenly Father

Contrast that young girl's letter to this one from a father who had experienced his own AHA and longed to see his own children return from the Distant Country.

*Dear Children,*

*You never quit being a parent. As a father, I think about all of you and wonder what your lives have become. I wonder whether I was the kind of father you needed and wonder if I truly represented the Father whose love is greater than all. As I look back over the years when you were young and still living at home, I see so many failures on my part. I see how I was such a poor example of our Father in heaven, whose love casts out all fear.*

*When I was growing up, my dad and I were not close. I saw him as someone who was ready to tell me how messed up I was every time I did something wrong. That mentality spilled over into my new life even after I became a follower of Jesus. For a long time I saw God much like I saw my dad. I struggled with my relationship with God because I thought He was always unhappy with me. I believed that deception too long.*

*My prayer has been that in spite of me, you three will come to see God for the loving Father that He is. He showed us how important we are to Him by sacrificing His only Son, Jesus, so we could be in a relationship with Him. He loves you far better than I ever could. I hope you will someday understand this deeply. I want you to know that I have always loved each of you. You are always important to me, and I will love you no matter what choices you make. I will pray until my dying breath that not one of you will be lost, but that each of you will open your hearts to Jesus and find the love I have finally found. Please forgive an old fool who chased after things that never truly fill a man. I am proud to be your dad.*

*With His love,*
*Dad*

God's true image is a heavenly Father who is reasonable, pleasable, merciful, and caring. His love extends beyond the boundaries of our comprehension. His efforts to reach and heal and know us broke the cosmic laws of life and death and changed the reality of the very universe for all eternity past, present, and future.

Our perceptions from life on this earth can get in the way or cloud our vision. But refocusing on our heavenly Father realigns our perspective. God's Word reminds us that He takes delight in us (Ps. 149:4), rejoices over us (Zeph. 3:17), hears and heals us (Ps. 30:2), and loves us lavishly as His children (1 John 3:1).

Even if we've turned our backs and walked away from God, He is a loving, merciful, gracious, and caring Father who wants to do more than just help us—He wants to save us. And His perfect love is more than able to do so.

## My AHA

How has your relationship with your earthly father shaped your view of your heavenly Father? Make a list in the left column of the characteristics of your father. Then look up and include Bible verses about God the Father and His faithfulness in the column on the right. Here's an example to get started:

| My father ... | But my heavenly Father ... |
|---|---|
| abandoned me and was never there. | "will never leave or forsake" me (Deut. 31:8). |
|  |  |

# DAY 4

## *Wake Up*

*And he said to me, "Son of man, listen carefully and take to heart all the words I speak to you."*

Ezekiel 3:10

Not long ago, one of my daughters set my phone alarm tone to match that of her favorite animal. It's labeled "Horses Neighing." It should be called "Death by Stampede." At five thirty in the morning, my alarm went off, and I shot straight up, wide awake—a stampede was charging through my bedroom.

While changing it back to my standard alarm, I noticed a wide array of other options. Some of the sounds wouldn't do anything to get me up, such as the one labeled "Harp." Try it on your iPhone. The soft trill just makes me sleepy. And "Doorbell" is just too confusing to wake up to.

The most effective alarm ringtone for me is "Old Car Horn." Think in terms of a house alarm that you can hear on the other side of the neighborhood. Now imagine that you are sleeping inside the speaker. It's highly effective. And it includes a backup if I somehow manage to sleep through it: my wife's foot kicking me to stop that awful noise.

But here's what I've discovered: the effectiveness of any alarm is in direct correlation to how much you don't want to hear it. In other words, until your desire to not hear the alarm outweighs your desire to keep sleeping—you're not going to wake up.

## Awakening

A similar sudden awakening takes place when God finally gets our attention. It's the first step in AHA. The alarm sounds, and this time we hear it. We immediately become aware of our present circumstances and the reality that something must change.

The Prodigal Son experienced this in Luke 15. After taking his inheritance money from his father, wasting it, and having to resort to feeding pigs, the Prodigal Son *"came to his senses."*

He sat straight up and suddenly realized what his life had become. When he ran away, he'd never thought his journey would have that ending. But life had gotten his attention, and he knew things had to change.

Have you ever had a moment like this? The Holy Spirit opens your eyes, and you see something that you had somehow missed before. You have a startling realization that changes everything.

Sometimes, awakening comes abruptly.

A man returns from a late-night casino binge to find his wife and kids gone. She's had enough of his lies and crushing debts. *The alarm sounds.*

A wife returns from a flirtatious meet-up with her high school sweetheart. She bumps a table and looks at the picture she has knocked over: she and her husband and three children are making funny faces. *The alarm sounds.*

A college student's grades arrive in the mall. His partying has flunked him out of school.

She's a junior in high school, and with trembling hands, she holds a pregnancy test, waiting for the result.

He logs off the website, deletes his history, and turns off the computer. His wife sleeps in the other room, but he has chosen this over her.

Sooner or later in the Distant Country, *the alarm will sound.*

# Heavy Sleeper

The son in Luke 15 didn't hear the alarm until he made it to the pigpen.

At every step in his story, there was some alarm that he could have—should have—heard: essentially wishing his father was dead, losing all his money, being abandoned by his "friends," encountering a famine, and going to work with the pigs. It's hard to read this story and not ask: "How did he not hear the alarm? How could he sleep through that?"

Often we miss the alarms sounding in our lives because we don't want to hear them. But chances are that if you're reading this book and seeking an AHA journey, you have a desire to awaken.

So here's my question: Are there alarms sounding in your life right now?

You don't have to hit rock bottom before you come to your senses. God often sends us warnings and alarms to get our attention. He did so for the nation of Israel in 2 Chronicles 36:15 as the people and their kings turned their backs on God: "And the LORD God of their fathers sent warnings to them by His messengers, rising up early and sending them" (NKJV).

The expression *rising up early* doesn't mean God got out of bed early. Rather, it is best understood as "taking action early." In this context, it means He sounded the alarm as quickly as the problems were perceived. And then we read that He warned "because He had compassion on His people."

God is a loving Father. Like any good parent, when He sees His child in danger, He warns the child of the coming consequences.

Are you listening?

## My AHA

What are the alarms in your life that you've been ignoring?

_____

_____

_____

_____

How have you been hitting snooze and telling yourself, *Just a little bit longer?*

_____

_____

_____

_____


What is your wake-up call? What does God want to awaken you from?


_____

_____

_____

_____

# DAY 5

## *Right Word at the Right Time*

*For the word of God is alive and active. Sharper
than any double-edged sword, it penetrates even
to dividing soul and spirit, joints and marrow; it
judges the thoughts and attitudes of the heart.*

Hebrews 4:12

A few years ago my family visited my parents for the holidays. They live on a quiet cul-de-sac where cars rarely come down the street. My four-year-old son, Kael, was riding his Big Wheel down the driveway. I stepped outside and saw a car coming down the street pretty fast. Kael needed to be warned that the car was coming.

I didn't think, *I've got a good thirty seconds before that car makes contact with my son. That's enough time to check my texts before I say something.*

I didn't smile and say, "Hey, buddy, there's a Ford SUV coming right for you. You might want to think about slowing down."

With a sense of urgency, I yelled, "Kael, stop right now!"

As soon as I perceived the danger, I warned him. That's what a loving father does.

## God Speaks

One of the ways God sounds the alarm is to send us His Word at just the right time. That's what He did for Cain, Adam and Eve's son. You're probably familiar with the story of Cain and Abel, but there is a warning to Cain in this story that I had never noticed before.

Abel was a shepherd, and Cain was a farmer. Abel was obedient to God's command and brought his first fruits. He brought a portion of the best of his flocks as an offering to God. But Cain gave God the leftovers from his fields.

When God saw this, He accepted Abel's offering and blessed him, but He rejected Cain's offering. Cain got angry and jealous of his brother. He was upset. Cain, the world's first son, was on the prodigal path to the Distant Country. God saw what was happening and sounded the alarm.

Genesis 4:6–7 says, "Then the LORD said to Cain, 'Why are you angry? Why is your face downcast? If you do what is right, will you not be accepted?'"

God, as a Father, said, "Listen close. It's not too late. I know right now you're feeling discouraged. I know things haven't turned out like you wanted, but *it's not too late*. You still have an opportunity here to do the right thing. If you'll just do the right thing, even though you don't feel like it, everything will be okay."

Then God issued a second alarm: "But if you do not do what is right, sin is crouching at your door; it desires to have you, but you must rule over it." Draw a line under this phrase: "sin is crouching at your door."

God painted a picture of Cain getting ready to open a door. If he opened it, he would find that on the other side is a decision that will destroy his family and devastate his life. God the Father saw the first son going toward the door, and He put a heavy hand on the door. He held it shut for a moment and, in essence, said: "Now wait a minute, Cain. Push Pause. You need to take a deep breath and recognize something. What is right behind this door has the power to destroy. It seeks to have you. Cain, you need to be really careful with what you do next."

The alarm sounded as God stepped back and let Cain choose for himself. Just like the father in Luke 15, God was not going to force His child to make the right decision. Any parent knows that as much as you may want to have that kind of control, eventually the kids have to decide for themselves.

Cain ignored the alarms and opened the door. He invited his brother out to the field and killed him. Cain sleepwalked right through the alarm, and everything came crashing down around him.

## Tuning In

As I have listened to people's AHA stories over the years, one of the questions I often ask is: Looking back, can you see how God tried to get your attention even though you didn't realize it?

I am completely convinced that part of the supernatural power of God's Word is that it often intersects with our lives when we are most desperate for the truth. Hebrews tells us it is "alive and active." Like a GPS system that gives us a heads-up when our exit is quickly approaching, God's Word speaks into our lives right when we need it the most. As we seek and study the Bible, we give the Holy Spirit opportunity to shape our thinking, guide us, and sound alarms when necessary. Digging into Scripture is our way of listening and tuning our ears to our Father's voice.

## My AHA

Tune in to God's voice today. Prayerfully open your Bible and read. Choose a book and set a time to read every day this week. Spend five minutes less on Facebook and five minutes more in God's Word.

# DAY 6

## *Words of a Friend*

*Wounds from a friend can be trusted,*
*but an enemy multiplies kisses.*

Proverbs 27:6

A few years back I took my family to see my in-laws in Kansas. They live on a farm out in the middle of nowhere.

My kids love the country. And for weeks leading up to the trip, my youngest daughter, Macy, talked about how she was going to catch a pet while we were on the farm. She was determined to catch some animal, name it, and bring it home as her pet.

My wife and I would tell Macy, "Okay, that's sweet, honey." Because we knew you can't just go out into the country and catch a pet.

Turns out we were wrong.

We were sitting and talking in the living room when my daughter came in announcing that she had caught a pet. "I caught a hamster! I caught a hamster!" she yelled excitedly.

"Oh, that's nice," I said. Then I realized, *There are no hamsters on the farm. Hamsters don't roam wild in Kansas. But maybe it's a mouse. That's probably it. She's caught a sweet, harmless little mouse. How cute.*

My daughter dragged me outside and over to a tall plastic container. My little girl was so excited as she reached inside and picked up a huge, dirty field rat. I didn't believe in R.O.U.S.'s[†] until that moment. She began to pet it, softly stroking its spine.

You could tell the rat had lost whatever battle took place. It looked exhausted and shocked.

"I love my new hamster," she said, continuing to pet the vermin.

My father-in-law, who is a farmer and wildlife biologist, got a bit riled up. He yelled at her to put the rat down because it carried diseases. Then he added, "We need to kill that thing."

---

† In case you're not a Christian, that's a *Princess Bride* reference.

That's when my daughter flipped out. "No, it's my pet! You can't kill my hamster! It's mine! I found it!"

I had to chase her down and forcibly take it away from her. Once I pried the rat from her hands, she fell apart. Tears streamed down her face as I took the big ol' rat and let him loose. For days she cried about the fact that I let her pet hamster go.

She wanted a pet so badly that she convinced herself that the rat was a hamster despite overwhelming evidence to the contrary. Even when some trusted people in her life tried to speak truth and impress reality upon her, she lashed out and continued to disagree.

Often we do the same.

That's why we need a friend whom we've given permission to tell us like it is—no matter what. Even if we refuse to listen at first, we all need a friend who will tell us when we're neglecting our family for work. A friend who will say something when our spending gets out of control. A friend who will challenge us to do more than just come to church a few weekends a month. A friend who will question a new relationship we're beginning.

Words from a friend like that can often be the most effective alarms in our lives. The Prodigal Son needed a friend like this, but in the Distant Country, I'm sure they were hard to find.

Proverbs 27:6 says, "Wounds from a friend can be trusted." And sometimes, in emergency life situations, a familiar voice speaking truth into your life is exactly what you need, even if you don't want it at the moment.

In Galatians 2, Paul wrote about the time when his friend and fellow apostle, Peter, withdrew from the Gentiles because he was afraid of criticism from the Jews. Paul recorded in Galatians 2:11 how he handled this: "When Cephas [Peter] came to Antioch, I opposed him to his face, because he stood condemned."

A good friend has your spiritual back. A good friend will sound the alarm. He or she may not want to say it. You may not want to hear it. But it may be the only way you'll wake up.

## My AHA

List the names of friends whom you have given permission to tell you the absolute truth. If you can't come up with anyone, consider who would be trustworthy to fill that role in your life.

_____

_____

_____

_____

_____

_____

Reach out today to foster this kind of honest relationship with a Christian leader or peer whose faith you admire and respect. List steps you can take toward building the friendship. Circle the one you will do today.

_____

_____

_____

_____

_____

_____

# DAY 7

## *Erasing Famines*

*And we know that in all things God works for the good of those who love him, who have been called according to his purpose.*

Romans 8:28

Try this hypothetical exercise. It was originally part of an experiment done by psychologist Jonathan Haidt. First read this life summary:

> Jillian will be born in August. As she grows, Jillian will develop a learning disability that will prevent her from learning to read at the appropriate age. Due to this disability, she will struggle with school for the rest of her years as a student. Despite her best efforts, her grades will always be average. In high school, Jillian

will become best friends with a girl named Megan. They will share secrets and be nearly inseparable for much of their junior year. But Megan will be diagnosed with a rare, aggressive form of cancer, and she will pass away just as senior year begins. Jillian will mourn the loss, and her grades will suffer for it.

She will attend a local community college, working a job and taking a small course load. The two-year program will take her three-and-a-half years to complete, and just before heading to a state school, Jillian will be involved in a drunk-driving accident. A drunk driver will hit her from behind, pushing her car into an intersection, where a family of three will swerve to avoid her. They will skid off the road, hit a tree, and their youngest son will die. Though the fault isn't hers, Jillian will blame herself for his death and spiral into a deep depression.

Eventually, she will make it to a state school, finish her degree, and get a job working for a food distributor. She will love her job. Just as a

promotion comes her way, an economic down-
turn will force the company to lay off much of
their management, which now includes Jillian.
In the devastated economic climate, Jillian will
struggle to get work, and eventually she will file
for bankruptcy, selling her house and moving
into a small studio apartment to make ends
meet. Though she will strive to get back on
her feet, the economy will make it increasingly
hard to do so, and she'll spend a few years living
month to month.

She will eventually find another job, but
due to her bankruptcy and season of unemployment, she won't be able to retire the way
she thought she would, nor will she ever
make as much as she used to. She will have
to work hard into her old age, piecing her life
back together.[1]

Now imagine that Jillian is your daughter. This is her
unavoidable life story. She hasn't been born yet, but she will be
soon, and this is where her life is headed.

But you have five minutes to edit her story.

With an eraser—or a pen or pencil to cross out—you can eliminate whatever you want out of her life.

What do you erase first?

## What's Best?

Most of us instinctively and frantically begin to erase the learning disability and the car accident and the financial challenges. We love our children and want them to live lives without those hardships, pains, and setbacks. We would all prefer our children's lives be free from pain and anguish.

But ask yourself: Is that really what's best?

Do we really think a privileged life of smooth sailing is going to make our kids happy? Has it for us? What if you erase a difficult circumstance that will wake them up to prayer? What if you erase a hardship that's going to show them how to be joyful in spite of any circumstance? What if you erase some pain and suffering that ends up being the catalyst God uses in their life to cause them to cry out to Him? What if you erase a difficult circumstance that wakes them up to God's purpose for their lives?

It may sound harsh, but the number one contributor to spiritual growth is not sermons, books, or small groups;

the number one contributor to spiritual growth is *difficult circumstances*.

I've seen this in personal experience, reading spiritual-growth surveys, and from talking to thousands of people over the years. AHA comes out of the suffering, setbacks, and challenges of life. Many people point to those moments as their greatest moments of spiritual awakening.

In Proverbs 20:30, the Bible basically says it sometimes takes a painful experience to make us change our ways. And sometimes it does.

Sometimes it takes cancer to awaken us to things of eternal value.

Sometimes it takes unemployment to awaken us to deeper prayer life.

Sometimes it takes a broken heart for us to finally let Jesus in.

None of us enjoy the difficult circumstances. They're hard. They hurt. And sometimes we do our best to roll over, cover our heads with a pillow, and go back to sleep to avoid them.

But difficult circumstances sound an alarm and give us an opportunity—an opportunity to wake up and encounter God in a deeper way than ever before. An opportunity to watch Him "work all things together for good." An opportunity to see God more clearly and to experience His healing, redemption, and restoration on a whole new level.

That kind of thinking runs contrary to everything we see in the world around us, but it's far more real. Carrying, guiding, and healing us through our pain and difficulty is exactly the kind of work God specializes in.

## My AHA

Recast your difficult circumstances as an underdog story. If you were making a movie of your story with God as producer, how would it go? Write or storyboard your tale.

_____

_____

_____

_____

_____

_____

_____

# DAY 8

## *Getting What We Deserve*

*Do not be deceived: God cannot be mocked.*
*A man reaps what he sows.*

Galatians 6:7

Alan Robertson is the oldest son of Phil and Kay Robertson and the beardless brother of the "Duck Dynasty" clan. He was a good kid growing up but was drawn to darker influences in his teen years.

> "I was hiding in plain sight. Inside I was not who I should have been."
>
> One night [Alan] Robertson and his buddies spent an evening drinking and tearing up some mailboxes.

The next day a knock on the door led to
a confession and a confrontation as Phil took
off his belt and whipped all the boys.

"A spanking was not going to change me,"
Robertson said. "Finally, a few months later
my dad said, 'Al, we love you, but the effect
you're having on the younger boys is bad. If
you're not willing to change, hit the road.'"

So Alan left home and headed to New Orleans. He joined
the large party scene and began dating a nurse who he believed
was divorced.

One Sunday morning Alan discovered the tires of his car
were flat. While he was still kneeling down to inspect them, a
man attacked him with a crowbar. Turned out the nurse was still
married.

Alan fought back and was able to escape. Police officers
arrived and apprehended the attacker after he took out the rest of
his fury on Alan's '76 Monte Carlo. But they had little sympathy
for Alan because he'd been sleeping with another man's wife.

One officer asked, "What are your parents
doing now?"

In an AHA moment, that question drew Robertson back to his home and family.

"I realized then that I could be home where Mom would be cooking a roast after church," Robertson said. "That was my awakening."

Robertson headed for home and pulled up to his parents' front yard where Miss Kay was waiting. He was hugging her when Phil came out. Robertson expected a lecture or at least a reminder of what he'd done, but Phil hugged him and said, "Welcome home."

"That hug meant so much to me," Robertson said. "That night, we had the fatted catfish. It felt like home."

Later, Robertson asked his dad to baptize him in the river.[1]

## You Asked for It

We're quick to demand justice in the lives of other people. *She got what she deserved*, we think—or say out loud like the police officers that helped Alan.

But it's a different story for ourselves. We want to do whatever we want to do without paying the price. And most of the time, we don't see the poor choices we are making in the moment—or we're skilled at conveniently ignoring the negative potential.

Eventually it all catches up with us—sometimes sooner, sometimes much later. But as the Bible says, "Do not be deceived: God cannot be mocked. A man reaps what he sows" (Gal. 6:7).

That's exactly what happened to the Prodigal Son. He spent all his money on wild living. That was no one else's fault. He arrived in the Distant Country and lived it up for a time; and after many nights of buying rounds and throwing parties, he was left with an empty wineglass *and* an empty wallet. The money was gone, and there was no one to blame but himself. His own actions and choices brought about consequences.

He found himself in a pigpen, so hungry he longed to fill his stomach with pig slop. If he hadn't left his father's house and hadn't blown all his money on wild living, he wouldn't have been in this position.

When you are in the Distant Country, it's only a matter of time before your decisions catch up to you. Those consequences spread like ripples on a still pond after a rock is thrown in. Your choices and actions are the cause, and they bring about effects.

God often brings us to a desperate moment through deserved consequences. The weight of possible consequences can help us look back on our poor choices with greater clarity. The moment the consequences of our decisions catch up to us, that is an invitation to cry out to God for help.

Don't wait for the consequences of your actions to come crashing down around you. Heed the warning signs. Wake up. And come back to the Father.

## *My AHA*

Where are your choices taking you? What's rippling through your life? What consequences are you causing? Take an honest look at what impact your actions are having—on yourself and others.

Fill out the following diagram. Start in the center of the circle by writing one of your regular actions, practices, or habits—maybe one that you like to keep secret or that causes conflict in your life. In the next ring, write three possible outcomes. Then trace ongoing possible results toward the outside of the circle. You can draw more circles to examine other actions.

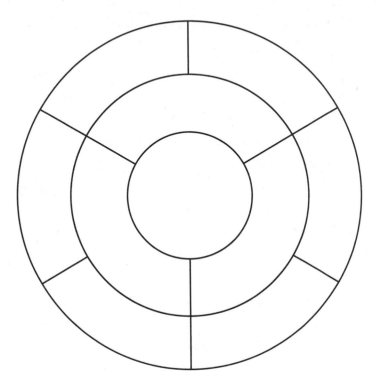

# DAY 9

## Redeeming the Pain

*The LORD is close to the brokenhearted and*
*saves those who are crushed in spirit.*

Psalm 34:18

Jerry Sittser was in a car accident several years ago. He and his family had driven to rural Idaho to experience a Native American powwow as part of his children's homeschooling lessons. On their way home after dark, a drunk driver slammed into them head-on. In the accident Jerry lost three generations. In one moment his family was obliterated. He lost his mom. He lost his wife. He lost his young daughter. He himself somehow walked away without physical injury, and his three other young children survived.

I recently caught part of a radio interview of Jerry talking about what it was like to experience such a major loss.

Eventually he wrote a book called *A Grace Disguised* in which he describes going through this difficult journey. In it, he wrote:

> Sooner or later all people suffer loss, in little doses or big ones, suddenly or over time, privately or in public settings. Loss is as much a part of normal life as birth, for as surely as we are born into this world we suffer loss before we leave it.
>
> It is not, therefore, the *experience* of loss that becomes the defining moment of our lives, for that is as inevitable as death, which is the last loss awaiting us all. It is how we *respond* to loss that matters. That response will largely determine the quality, the direction, and the impact of our lives.
>
> This book is not intended to help anyone get over or even through the experience of catastrophic loss, for I believe that "recovery" from such loss is an unrealistic and even harmful expectation, if by recovery we mean resuming the way we lived

and felt prior to the loss. Instead, the book is intended to show how it is possible to live in and be enlarged by loss, even as we continue to experience it. That is why I will emphasize the power of response. Response involves the *choices* we make, the *grace* we receive, and ultimately the *transformation* we experience in the loss.[1]

Did you catch that wisdom? The defining moment can be *our response* to the loss.

Our story may include loss, but ultimately our story doesn't have to be a story about loss. AHA is about how we respond to the loss and let God shape our story.

# Like Job

Job may be the most famous example of loss and suffering in the world. Even people who don't believe in the Bible know that Job endured catastrophic loss.

In the Old Testament book of Job, Satan was betting on the fact that Job would respond to difficult circumstances by distancing himself from God. Job was living what most of us would call the good life. He was a wealthy man with a large estate and a large family.

But Job faced one difficult circumstance after another. He lost his children when a strong wind knocked down a house that collapsed on top of them. He was afflicted with painful sores from the soles of his feet to the top of his head. He lost everything. His wealth, his children, his health—it all disappeared. His wife had seen enough. In Job 2:9, she said to him, "Are you still maintaining your integrity? Curse God and die!" But in the midst of the pain, Job experienced an awakening. At the end of the book, he said to God: "My ears had heard of you but now my eyes have seen you" (42:5).

*AHA.*

In the midst of tremendous pain, Job saw God more clearly. In his disappointment, he didn't distance himself from God; instead, he drew nearer.

## Draw Nearer

I know there are people reading this right now who are experiencing difficult circumstances. In your pain and disappointment, there is part of you that wants to turn from God or continue walking away. The Distant Country may seem like it offers relief. But don't waste the pain. Hear the alarm and wake up.

In 2 Corinthians 7:10 we read, "For God sometimes uses sorrow in our lives to help us turn away from sin and seek eternal life" (TLB). It doesn't say "God causes"; it says "God uses," and He wants to use these circumstances to draw you closer to Him.

He is big enough and loving enough to carry you through the pain.

David told us, "The LORD is close to the brokenhearted and saves those who are crushed in spirit" (Ps. 34:18). God said to Isaiah, "As a mother comforts her child, so will I comfort you" (Isa. 66:13). He told Jeremiah, "I will turn their mourning into gladness; I will give them comfort and joy instead of sorrow" (Jer. 31:13).

God is not a distant, uncaring god. He is a loving Father offering comfort, peace, and transformation. He waits with open arms to those who are hurting.

The question is: When difficult circumstances come your way, when there is a famine in the land like that encountered by the Prodigal Son, how will you respond? How are you responding? If you let Him, God will use those circumstances to wake you up and ultimately draw you closer to Him.

Every hurt or discouragement, from the inconvenient to the catastrophic, is an opportunity on the AHA journey to draw nearer to God—to experience His transformation within and through us. In a sense, it's the chance to choose your own ending. What will define your story?

## *My AHA*

List any hurts or losses you are facing or have faced, followed by your responses.

_____

_____

_____

_____

_____

_____

What pattern do you see? What steps will you take to redefine your story?

# DAY 10

## *Escaping the Country of the Blind*

*Open my eyes that I may see
wonderful things in your law.*
Psalm 119:18

The British author H. G. Wells is most famous for his science fiction novels such as *The War of the Worlds*, *The Invisible Man*, and *The Time Machine*. But he also wrote short stories, including one called "The Country of the Blind."

It's a story about a fictional village in Ecuador, nestled high within the Andes. This village had been cut off from the rest of the world and long forgotten. And in this place, everyone in the village was blind.

The blindness had begun long ago due to a disease that caused all the children to be born blind, and it had continued through more than fifteen generations.

One day a lost mountain climber stumbled into the village. He had fallen down a remote peak and miraculously survived without major injury.

It didn't take the climber long to discover that he was the only one in the valley who had sight. No one even understood the concept of sight or had any idea of what seeing meant. These people had long forgotten what it was like to see the majestic mountains around them or the sun washing the clouds with color overhead. There were no descriptions passed along through the ages of what it might be to see. It was not something they understood. The people had no explanation for what their shriveled eyes were or why they were there.

Initially the foreigner tried to describe sight to them and help them understand the concept of sight. But every effort was futile. They didn't understand. In fact, they thought he was crazy and defective. If this man wanted to stay in this land, something had to be done.

And the man wanted to stay. There was a young lady there who had stolen his heart. But a marriage to this insane foreigner was unacceptable to her father and the rest of the village—unless ...

A doctor there felt confident he could cure the man with a simple surgery to remove the man's eyes. It was his eyes, after all, that were affecting this man's brain, the doctor declared. And everyone in the village said, "Thank heaven for science." The surgery was scheduled.

On the day of his surgery, the man went for a walk. He simply planned to go to a lonely place where the meadows were beautiful and wait until the hour of his procedure. "But as he walked he lifted up his eyes and saw the morning, the morning like an angel in golden armour, marching down the steeps," Wells wrote. "It seemed to him that before this splendour he and this blind world in the valley, and his love and all, were no more than a pit of sin."[1]

So the man kept walking, and he looked up at the mountains with renewed vision and began to see gullies and chimneys where he could climb back through the towering gorge. And soon the man who could see escaped the country of the blind.

# Escape

We live in the country of the blind. We experience awakening. God opens our eyes. We're able to see, but it doesn't take long to realize that there are people all around us who think we really need to be cured of our sight.

We come to church on weekends, and our eyes are opened and conviction comes in our hearts. We know God has spoken to us, but Monday comes and we find ourselves back in the country of the blind. Everyone thinks we're a little bit crazy; we've taken this too far; and what would really be best is if we would go back to being blind.

Or you come back from church camp after a spiritual awakening. Things are going to be different. But you find yourself in the country of the blind, and the people all around want to cure you of your sight.

This is where we live. And we must continually open our eyes. We must refocus on the heights above and press toward the beauty where God wants to draw us.

We must continue to pray David's prayer, that God would open our eyes—each day—so that we might see what God wants us to see even in this country of the blind.

## My AHA

Change your perspective. Plan a retreat. Block off a weekend on your calendar. Or a day. Or an hour, if that's all you can do. The key is to break out of your routine. The goal is to go somewhere to look and to listen, to seek the Scripture, to open your eyes and refocus on your heavenly Father. Start now with a walk around your block, and pray as you go.

# DAY 11

## *Let Go of Regret*

*There is now no condemnation for those who are in Christ Jesus, because through Christ Jesus the law of the Spirit who gives life set you free from the law of sin and death.*

Romans 8:1–2

Jesus begins the parable of the prodigal son like this: "There was a man who had two sons. The younger one said to his father, 'Father, give me my share of the estate.' So he divided his property between them" (Luke 15:11–12).

It doesn't sound newsworthy when we read it. But in the patriarchal, family-centered, honor-based culture of Jesus's time, you did *not* ask your father for your inheritance early. In effect, the younger son was saying, "I wish you were already dead, Dad." In fact, the Greek term for "property" used in verse 12, *ton bion*, literally means "the life." A father gave a son life and livelihood through an inheritance. So essentially, this son is asking for his father's life.

Shockingly, the father complies. The eldest son always received a double portion of the inheritance, so this younger brother got about one-third of his father's total estate. The fact that the father is willing to grant this disrespectful, selfish demand is our first clue that this is no ordinary father. And those listening to Jesus would have found it hard to believe that any father would comply with such a request.

The inheritance the son received was in all likelihood mostly land, so when Luke 15:13 says that he "got together all he had" and left, it likely means that he sold the land he was given and took the money. If it wasn't bad enough that he told his father he wished he were dead, it's an even bigger assault on the family's dignity that the younger son sold his family's land to someone else. So one-third of the land on which the father and older son are living now belongs to a stranger. If the father wasn't insulted, embarrassed, and stripped of his dignity before, surely he is now.

## What Have I Done?

With awakening often comes regret. Once our eyes are opened to the wake of pain trailing behind us, it's normal to think,

*What have I done?* It's easy to see how the Prodigal Son would have felt such regret, but what about the father? What memories haunted him? What scenes replayed in his head of happy times past and moments he wished he could change? On those long, bleak days of mourning his son's departure and waiting for his unlikely return, this patriarch must have asked the universal questions of a parent:

> *What could I have done differently? How could*
> *I have stopped him? Where did I go wrong?*

But maybe Jesus's silence on these details holds an AHA, especially for the parents of a prodigal. Just as Jesus knew what His listeners would have culturally understood in the day that He told this parable, He knows what every parent throughout history feels to their marrow. He understands the loss, the embarrassment, the confusion. He knows more deeply than we can imagine the sting of rejection from those He has poured out His life for. Maybe you know it too. Maybe you've experienced it firsthand or seen it in a loved one. Maybe you've felt the regret that the son eventually came to experience as he suffered in the Distant Country. Or maybe you understand the pain and regret of this father:

*My dear prodigal son,*

*Though I thought I knew everything about unconditional love, it was you who allowed me to practice what I preached. As you have suffered through some dark days and painful losses, I have suffered along with you.*

*I know you have rejected God for many years. I know you yearn for something bigger than yourself. I know underneath all that bravado and self-assurance is a good heart and you would like to believe in something. You ask your brother's friends about God too often for me not to have some hope.*

*And so with a heavy heart and tears in my eyes, I confess I am to blame for not taking you to church after your mother left. I pray you will forgive me. I pray you know that whatever capacity I have to love, it comes from the One who loved us enough to die for both of us. I will pray for you daily until the day I die, and I hope you know that you can always come to Jesus. He has always loved you and He always will. So do I.*

*Dad*

But this pain wasn't the point of Jesus's story. He knows there is much, much more waiting on the other side of AHA. He sees beyond the despair. He can redeem every failure. He can heal every regret. He can restore every sinner no matter how far we have wandered. And he can repair every strained and broken relationship.

## My AHA

What regrets are weighing you down—as a prodigal, as a parent, as a person? What shame is holding you back? List below your regrets and any shame you are feeling as you prayerfully exchange your condemnation for God's forgiveness and healing. Consider making your list on a separate paper. Then crumple it up and dispose of it—in the trash or a fireplace—as a tangible sign of release.

_____

_____

_____

_____

_____

_____

# DAY 12

## *In Plain Sight*

*Then you will know the truth, and the truth will set you free.*
John 8:32

Charlie and Carol Gasko enjoyed their retired life in palm-tree-lined Santa Monica, California. The couple lived two blocks from the beach. They would walk holding hands and stop to pet people's dogs. Occasionally they would dine at Michael's, a fine-dining establishment down the street, but they always preferred the same table tucked away in a back corner of the patio.

Come to think of it, the Gaskos were pretty private people. They did help their eighty-eight-year-old neighbor carry groceries sometimes. Another neighbor described the eighty-one-year-old Charlie as kind and Carol, sixty, as sweet. But the couple mostly kept to themselves and would never answer the phone. It was clear they had their boundaries.

Charlie and Carol seemed like any ordinary retirees.

Until one day in 2011 when the FBI closed in and arrested them both.

Turns out Charlie and Carol were really James "Whitey" Bulger and Catherine Elizabeth Greig. He was a notorious East Coast mobster who shared space on the FBI's Most Wanted list alongside Osama bin Laden. Bulger had been Boston's most feared mob boss from the late 1970s to the mid '90s, and he faced charges for nineteen brutal murders. He had been on the lam for sixteen years.

"It's like finding out your grandparents are murderers," a neighbor told reporters.[1]

Bulger and his longtime girlfriend were hiding in plain sight.

But in one moment, their charade had ended. Their bluff was called. And the truth was revealed.

## Revealed

Have you ever had a moment when the Holy Spirit opens your eyes, and you see something you had somehow missed before?

You have a startling realization that changes everything. A truth is revealed that makes everything clear.

Walking the AHA journey is filled with continual moments of awakening as we seek God in our lives. Sometimes we're looking for awakening. Sometimes it takes us by surprise.

Sometimes the awakening is right there in plain sight, waiting for us to let God realign our vision. Sometimes it's not even our circumstances that change—just the way we see them.

That's the way it was for one father who told me about praying for his daughter for seven years—her whole life— that God would use her in a powerful way. At the same time, for the past three years, he had been asking God to heal her from life-threatening cancer. Her illness gave her opportunities to tell many doctors and nurses about her faith in Jesus. Several of her extended family members had started coming to church as a direct result of seeing the supernatural strength with which she battled her illness. One night the father prayed the same prayer he had prayed her whole life—that God would use her powerfully—but when he prayed that God would heal her completely, he came to such a startling realization it was like he could almost hear God asking him,

"Well, which one do you want? You have prayed her entire life for her to be an awesome witness, and now she is."

Jesus put it this way: "Then you will know the truth, and the truth will set you free" (John 8:32).

Have you had some moments like this? Moments when you realized something you never have before? Moments when you realized the truth and tasted freedom?

You realize you've been trying to live out the Christian life from your own power and strength rather than out of the power of the Holy Spirit.

You realize you weren't actually following Jesus; you were just following a list of rules and rituals.

You realize the reason you struggle with food is that you are trying to satisfy your soul by filling your stomach.

You realize you've put incredible pressure on your romantic relationship, because you've been looking to your significant other to do for you what only God can do for you.

You realize you are stressed out about money, because you're putting your trust in money instead of in God.

You realize you've spent so much of your life wrestling with guilt and shame, because you thought being good enough would save you, instead of relying on the grace of God to save you.

That truth has always been true, but for some reason you just didn't see it before. Like the Prodigal Son, you were in the right place at the right time, and finally a startling realization woke you up and brought you to your senses.

Look for the right time. Ask God to make His message clear.

## My AHA

Write a brief story of a startling realization you have experienced. Ask God to show you what's hiding in plain sight in your life.

# DAY 13

## Seek the Silence

*Be still, and know that I am God.*

Psalm 46:10

Have you ever had a moment when the Holy Spirit opens your eyes and you see something that somehow you had missed before?

The Prodigal Son's startling realization happened when it dawned on him that, "Many of my father's hired servants have food to spare, and here I am starving to death!" (Luke 15:17).

For the Prodigal Son to finally make this startling realization, he had to have some time alone. Some time to think. My guess is that this was the first time in a long time that he had sat in silence.

Even then, it wasn't his choice. He ran out of money. His friends bailed on him. A famine swept over the land. He was driven to the pigpen. There was no one to talk to. There was nothing to distract him. He was alone in the Distant Country, forced away from the noise of wild living and from the party crowd. No more staying up into the early hours of morning and sleeping in late without time for sober thinking and reflection.

# Turning Down Distraction

To seek AHA, to discover awakening, you begin with some solitude and silence. You may find that God has been trying to get your attention for a while, but you haven't been able to hear Him. Not because He hasn't been loud enough, but because you haven't been quiet enough.

It's as though you've been at home watching a game. You have the TV turned up fairly loud, but someone is using the blender in the kitchen, someone else is running the vacuum cleaner in the living room, and one of the kids has a radio cranked up down the hallway. You think, *I just need to turn up the volume*. So you grab the remote to turn the television volume even louder, only to find that it's already turned up all the way. But you still can't hear the game.

What's the problem? The problem isn't the volume. The problem is that you need to turn down the interfering noises.

# Alone on the Mountain

When God speaks to us, He often speaks in solitude and silence. That's when we tend to have a startling realization. It tends to play out a little bit more as it did with the prophet Elijah in 1 Kings 19.

Elijah went to a mountain to meet with God, but God hadn't showed up yet. While Elijah was waiting, a strong wind blew through the area, and Elijah thought, *Oh, God must be in that wind.* But the wind died down, and God was not in the wind.

Then there was an earthquake that shook the whole mountain, and Elijah thought, *God's in the earthquake.* That's how we would expect God to get our attention. But God was not in the earthquake.

Then there was this fire that swept through the area, and Elijah thought, *Well, God must be in the fire.* But the fire subsided, and God was not in the fire.

And then the Bible tells us that God spoke to Elijah in a gentle whisper. But the literal translation here speaks of a sound that is even quieter than a whisper. The NRSV translates God's voice as being: "a sound of sheer silence" (v. 12). That's when Elijah hears from the Lord.

For many of us, a little silence and solitude are the only things standing between us and a startling realization.

Do you have some quiet moments set aside in the busyness of your life? God says, "Be still, and know that I am God" (Ps. 46:10). I like this definition of stillness: silence on the outside and surrender on the inside.

To find stillness, we must turn down or distance ourselves from the distractions around us.

## My AHA

Set aside some time for stillness today. Put it on your calendar. Go on—complete with a reminder alarm. Start your time reading Psalm 46 and meditating on it.

# DAY 14

## *Willing to Listen*

*The way of fools seems right to them, but the wise listen to advice.*

Proverbs 12:15

Sometimes the startling realization only takes place when someone else steps in with a healthy perspective. It's as if he or she flips a switch that illuminates a cartoonlike lightbulb above our heads. Suddenly we get it when someone boldly tells us the truth.

Naaman was an army commander in the Bible who desperately needed someone to flip the switch. But he had to find the humility to listen.

## Mighty Expectations

Naaman was a successful, high-ranking military official for the king of Aram. In 2 Kings 5, he's described as a brave warrior.

But Naaman's life started to fall apart when he was afflicted with a horrible skin disease.

During his raids on Israel, Naaman had captured a young Israelite girl to serve his wife. And this servant had an idea: "If only my master could meet the prophet of Samaria, he would be healed of his skin disease" (2 Kings 5:3 MSG).

There was no cure for leprosy in that day, so Naaman didn't have any other options. He got the king's blessing to go meet this prophet named Elisha and set out to be healed.

He didn't travel light. Naaman's entourage included horses and chariots, clothes and supplies, including "750 pounds of silver, 150 pounds of gold, and ten sets of clothes" (v. 5 MSG). Clearly, Naaman had come prepared to earn his healing, no matter what the prophet would order. A quest to the edge of Israel? Bring it on. A specific mountain to climb or a people to conquer? No problem. Naaman was ready for whatever the prophet would throw at him—except, of course, Elisha's curveball response.

Elisha's instructions were, "Go to the River Jordan and immerse yourself seven times. Your skin will be healed and you'll be as good as new" (v. 10 MSG).

Sounds simple enough, right?

Elisha had insulted Naaman in every way possible with this message. Naaman arrived at Elisha's door with his caravan, and the prophet didn't even come outside to greet him. Instead, he sent a messenger. Naaman was not the kind of guy who received messengers. He *sent* messengers.

So Naaman stormed off in a huff and complained, "I thought he'd personally come out and meet me, call on the name of GOD, wave his hand over the diseased spot, and get rid of the disease" (v. 11).

Naaman had pictured this going down a certain way. He'd expected the prophet to display some pomp and circumstance. On top of that, Naaman was not going to debase himself in an Israeli river. He continued complaining, "The Damascus rivers, Abana and Pharpar, are cleaner by far than any of the rivers in Israel. Why not bathe in them? I'd at least get clean" (v. 12).

Naaman sulked. He needed an AHA. Unless he had a startling realization, he wouldn't be healed. He needed someone to flip the switch, but who?

A servant approached the sulking commander and said, "Father, if the prophet had asked you to do something hard and heroic, wouldn't you have done it? So why not this simple 'wash and be clean'?" (v. 13).

The servant pointed out a simple truth. Naaman came ready for an epic adventure or a grand healing ceremony. He came prepared to pay any price for his healing. So why not just wash? In the nicest way possible, this servant said, "Get over yourself and take a bath."

The words came from a lowly source. Naaman could have kept up his arrogance, but he allowed himself to listen. And he experienced a startling realization. Immediately, Naaman went down to the Jordan and washed seven times. God cleansed him of his disease, and he returned to Elisha to articulate his awakening. In verse 15, Naaman declared, "I now know beyond a shadow of a doubt that there is no God anywhere on earth other than the God of Israel."

## Humble to Hear

Often we are the last ones to see the hard truth in our own lives. It's right in front of us, but somehow we miss it. We all need someone in our life who can tell it like it is. But Naaman's story reminds us that sometimes it takes humility to listen.

Sometimes the words of truth come from an unlikely source—or a "simpler" source. For Naaman it was a servant.

For you, maybe it's a child saying, "Daddy, can we play?"

Maybe it's an employee saying, "Are you all right?"

Regardless of the source, it takes humility to listen, especially when the truth is hard.

Maybe it's a close friend saying, "I've been worried about you lately."

Maybe it's a parent saying, "We need to talk."

Maybe it's a spouse saying, "You were wrong."

Listening—being willing to listen—is a key component of AHA. We must be willing to listen to God and to those in our life who will give us godly advice.

We may not always like what we hear at first. Our natural reaction may be to ignore it or to defend ourselves. But AHA often comes in the hard truth when we're willing to lay aside our pride and listen.

## My AHA

Want to know the truth? Want to really know the hard truth? Ask your spouse, closest friend, parent, or a trusted leader what blind spot needs some attention in your life. Write down their guidance or advice here.

_____

_____

_____

_____

_____

# DAY 15

## *Honest with Myself*

*Nothing in all creation is hidden from God's sight.*
*Everything is uncovered and laid bare before the*
*eyes of him to whom we must give account.*

Hebrews 4:13

In January 2013 Lance Armstrong sat down with Oprah Winfrey as cameras rolled.

"Did you ever take banned substances to enhance your cycling performance?" Oprah asked.

"Yes," Armstrong answered.[1]

And so began the confession of the seven-time Tour de France winner, founder and chairman of the board of his cancer-fighting Livestrong Foundation, and transcendent sports celebrity.

Even in an era of public scandal, Armstrong's fall was one of the biggest. For years he had defended his innocence and gone to great lengths to crush his critics. But slowly and steadily the evidence mounted. Finally Armstrong was cornered, and he came clean in his interview with Oprah.

Was Armstrong's confession sincere? Was he truly sorry? Would he be a changed man?

Only Lance knows, and only time will reveal how the experience will change him.

## Regret or Repentance?

Lance Armstrong is not alone. Public failures and apologies have become common in our culture. Each of us could rattle off a long list of actors, athletes, politicians, business leaders, and other public figures whose misdeeds and confessions have been highly public.

In the book *The Art of the Public Grovel*, Susan Wise Bauer makes a helpful distinction between an apology and a confession: "An apology is an expression of regret: *I am sorry.* A confession is an admission of fault: *I am sorry because I did wrong. I sinned.*"[2]

That kind of confession is needed to get past awakening to the second ingredient of AHA: brutal honesty. We see it in Luke 15 after the Prodigal Son came to his senses. Verse 17 in the New Living Translation reads: "He said to himself."

There was no one else around. It was just him and the pigs. Sometimes the hardest conversation to have is the one you have with yourself. Brutal honesty begins when we look in the mirror and speak the truth about what we see. AHA requires you to tell the truth about yourself *to* yourself.

# Beyond Busted

As a pastor, it's not unusual for me to talk to someone who comes to confess a sin or some kind of ongoing struggle. When I sit down with that person, there are often tears as he or she admits the truth. I know it's a difficult and humbling thing to do, because I have been in that seat many times. But one of the questions I've learned to ask is, "Are you confessing this to me because you got caught?"

This is almost always the case.

> A husband found the email correspondence, and the emotional affair was undeniable.
> His parents found a joint in the floorboard of the car.
> The boss finally fired the alcoholic for coming to work drunk.

She couldn't pay her credit-card bills, and a
court case was brewing.
The college grades were finally posted, and
partying had taken its toll.
A pregnancy test came back positive, and she
wasn't sure who the father was.
His daughter walked in and saw what he was
looking at on the computer.

More often than not, the confessions I hear are motivated
by discovery. Just because they were caught doesn't mean the
honesty isn't sincere, but it makes it more difficult to know if
I'm listening to regret or repentance.

If you're a parent, you've probably seen this in your children. If you catch your child with his hand in the proverbial,
or literal, cookie jar, he may say, "I'm sorry." But is the apology honest? Is the child sorry for getting a cookie without
permission, or is the child sorry for getting caught? Usually
the child is just sorry he didn't have a better plan to heist the
cookies.

The honesty that's part of AHA is more than a simple
acknowledgment; it's a kind of brokenness. When there is
recognition but no repentance, AHA doesn't happen. You can

tell the person who caught you that you are sorry, but you must go beyond that. In an honest moment when no one else is around, you must tell yourself the truth about yourself and know that you are sorry.

That's the difference between regret and repentance.

Have you followed up an awakening by being brutally honest with yourself?

## My AHA

Answer these questions. If you can't bring yourself to write the answers, go into a bathroom, close the door, look in the mirror, and speak the honest truth. Some of these won't apply to you, but I hope they will move you to ask yourself some relevant, hard questions.

1.  Did you spend more time this week on Facebook or in prayer?

2.  When was the last time you told someone, "I love you"?

3.  How specifically have you helped someone in need in the last month?

4. When was the last time you said to someone, "I was wrong. Please forgive me"?

5. What's on your DVR at home? Your computer's history?

6. When was the last time you prayed with your spouse? With your children?

7. Can you name one missionary whom you pray for?

8. What sin have you not confessed to God or anyone else?

9. When was the last time you sat with an open Bible?

10. Did you spend more money this month eating out than on advancing the kingdom of God?

11. When was the last time you cried over your sin?

12. Who besides God knows about your secret sin?

# DAY 16

## *Honesty That Brings Healing*

*Whoever conceals their sins does not prosper, but the
one who confesses and renounces them finds mercy.*
Proverbs 28:13

Even though the world is now familiar with the Rwandan
genocide that took place in 1994, the atrocities are still
unimaginable to us and the brutality too difficult to compre-
hend. In a span of one hundred days, more than one million
ethnic Tutsis were slaughtered. Men, women, and children
were slain—mostly hacked to death by Hutu neighbors wield-
ing machetes. Evil ran amok.

Twenty years later, anyone who lived through the
bloodbath carries scars—many physical, all emotional. Alice
Mukarurinda lost her right hand and her baby daughter in
the killings. Emmanuel Ndayisaba was the man who took

both. He left Alice for dead in a swamp where she had been hiding.

Today Alice and Emmanuel are neighbors, coworkers, and friends.

Guilt gnawed at Emmanuel after the genocide. Two years later he turned himself in and confessed his murders. He served six years in prison and was then freed when the president pardoned all Hutus who admitted their guilt.

Emmanuel joined a weekly group of genocide killers and survivors. It was the same group Alice attended. Emmanuel avoided his victim at first, but eventually he kneeled before her and asked for forgiveness. After a couple weeks of prayerful consideration, Alice agreed to forgive.

Today the two both work for the same organization that builds houses for genocide survivors.

"Guilt is heavy," Alice told the Associated Press. "When one realizes how heavy it is the first thing they do to recuperate themselves is apologize."[1]

## The Next Step of Honesty

Many Rwandans have experienced AHA. Their pain is deep, and their journey has been difficult. But they have pursued and understood grace, forgiveness, and healing in a visceral way. They have also experienced the power of brutal honesty—including its next step.

Brutal honesty includes telling the truth about yourself to someone else.

The Prodigal Son understood that there was no way around it. After telling the truth to himself about his situation and what he deserved, he realized he also needed to be honest with his father. In Luke 15:18, he said: "I will set out and go back to my father and say to him: Father, I have sinned against heaven and against you."

He recognized that it wasn't enough for him to be honest with himself; he also needed to be honest with his father. Most of us don't practice voluntary confession. Not when it comes to being honest with ourselves, especially not when it comes to confessing to others. Voluntary confession is when we regularly and voluntarily acknowledge our sin and honestly admit our weaknesses to someone in our lives.

In 1 John 1:9, the Bible tells us that when we confess our sins to God, "He is faithful and just to forgive us our sins and to cleanse us from all unrighteousness." The Bible also says that Jesus took the punishment we deserve upon

Himself when He died on the cross. Jesus died for my sins, so that when I confess them, God forgives them.

Usually, we tell ourselves that it doesn't have to go any further than that: "If I'm honest with myself and with God, that's enough." But AHA requires more. In James 5:16, we read: "Therefore confess your sins to each other and pray for each other so that you may be healed."

When we are honest with God about our sins, He forgives us, but when we are honest with others, we find healing.

## Healing

What does *healing* mean?

The practice of confessing our sins to one another holds us accountable and helps us find the encouragement we need to break the cycle of our struggle. When we take what we've kept in the dark and drag it kicking and screaming into the light, we find that it loses much of its power over us.

And the healing James talks about is more literal than you might think. Check this out: A secular contemporary psychology textbook titled *Coping with Stress* confirms the healing power of confession. The author claims that "people who tend to keep secrets have more physical and mental complaints, on average, than people who do not ... [including] greater anxiety, depression, and bodily symptoms, such as back pain and headaches.... The initial embarrassment of confessing is frequently outweighed by the relief that comes with the verbalization of the darker, secretive aspects of the self."[2]

Like the Prodigal Son, you may need to be honest with the person you've offended or sinned against. Chances are you've already thought of a dozen excuses for why this isn't necessary, but the more you protest internally, the more likely it is you need sit down with him or her and talk.

## My AHA

Tell someone else. It's time to come clean. You can outline what you want to say here ...

_____

_____

_____

_____

_____

# DAY 17

## *Turn Off Denial*

*Here I am starving to death!*
Luke 15:17

My wife and I recently watched a news-magazine show that featured a reporter visiting different hotels. Black light in hand, the reporter would walk into one of the rooms, and the purple glow of his truth-detecting light would illuminate all manner of germs and stains in the room, bright neon against the bedspread. This is the surest way I know for a husband to ruin all future romantic getaways with his wife.

In one scene, the reporter waited in the lobby for a victim. He finally cornered a poor, unsuspecting couple—probably enjoying what had thus far been a great vacation—and asked if they would submit their room to his black-light experiment. My wife and I were involuntarily talking to the TV at this point: "Don't do it! This is going to ruin your anniversary! Run away now!"

Sadly, the couple agreed to take the crew up to their room. So the husband and wife, and the reporter and his camera crew, all crowded into the elevator and made small talk. The reporter held back any indication that he knew what would happen. They got to the room and walked in with the lights on. Everything looked pristine, as if room service had just been there. My wife and I commented on the cleanliness of the room, the crispness of the bedsheets.

This could be the one room that survived the test.

Suddenly, the lights went out and there was a moment of silence like you might expect in a movie just before the monster was revealed. The black light came on, and stains showed up everywhere. Unbelievably, it was even worse than the rooms shown previously. The neon glow was everywhere, including a suspiciously large stain on the carpet. As my wife and I groaned, we heard the couple start to panic. The wife began to scream, "Turn that off! Turn that off! Turn that off!"

After a few seconds, she rushed over to turn the lights back on. In an instant, everything looked normal again. She started to calm down and laughed nervously. "That's better," she said.

But, umm … here's the thing—*the stains were still there.*

The couple could no longer see them, but that didn't change the reality of the stains' existence.

# Denial

The word for this is *denial.* Denial is turning off the black light in an effort to make the stains disappear. You pretend everything is okay even though everything is not okay. Sigmund Freud defined denial this way: a defense mechanism in which a person is faced with a fact that is too uncomfortable to accept, so they reject it despite overwhelming evidence.

Instead of brutal honesty, many of us choose denial. When we are confronted with a reality that is so uncomfortable, so inconvenient, we choose to continue living in a false reality.

I read about another example of denial. What do you think is the number one way people respond when they get a bill in the mail that they don't have the money to pay? They don't open it.

The truth is too uncomfortable, so they pretend everything is okay. This is the same reason why women who have a family history of breast cancer are sometimes the least likely to get a mammogram, or why men who have a family history of heart disease often ignore the warning signs. The evidence may be there—it may be overwhelming—but our response is: *"Turn that off!"*

# Define Reality

We don't know how long it took the Prodigal Son to wake up and recognize the reality of his situation. He landed this awful job, but he made no changes to his life. He got to the point of wanting to eat pig slop but still didn't make any changes. He stuck with that job for a while, despite the overwhelming evidence that things had gone terribly wrong.

What keeps a person in the pigpen? *Denial.*

Even though you're feeding pig slop to pigs;

even though your spouse has filed for divorce;

even though you haven't been sober for a week in years;

even though you make yourself the same promise every night;

even though you can't remember the last time you got on your knees and prayed …

you keep living like everything is going to be okay.

Notice in the parable what the younger son finally gets honest about. He says in Luke 15:17, "Here I am starving to death!"

He defines the reality of his circumstances. The word *reality* could be defined as "the state of things as they actually exist."

But many of us get stuck in denial. We have an awakening, but we lack the courage to be brutally honest with ourselves about our current reality.

Doing so might be humiliating.

It's embarrassing.

It's painful.

*It's essential.*

## My AHA

Look around. What is the state of things as they actually exist in your life? Define the reality of your circumstances. Use pictures or icons if you're artistically inclined.

_____

_____

_____

_____

_____

_____

_____

# DAY 18

## *One Step at a Time*

*David sent someone to find out about her.*

2 Samuel 11:3

Bernie Madoff was big news several years ago. Over his long and distinguished financial career, Madoff had helped launch the NASDAQ stock market and advised the Securities and Exchange Commission. Then the seventy-year-old financier was convicted of running the biggest fraudulent scheme in US history.

For decades Madoff conned investors out of $65 million, before getting caught in 2008. Madoff's elaborate Ponzi scheme fell apart when his clients requested $7 billion back and he simply didn't have enough to give. The game was up.

How could this well-respected investment leader whom so many people trusted have deceived them so badly? At the end of his well-publicized trial, Madoff made a statement—an apology—that offered some insight into how he ended up a criminal. Madoff said:

> I believed when I started this problem, this crime, that it would be something I would be able to work my way out of, but that became impossible. As hard as I tried, the deeper I dug myself into a hole. I made a terrible mistake, but it wasn't the kind of mistake that I had made time and time again, which is a trading mistake. In my business, when you make a trading error, you're expected to make a trading error, it's accepted. My error was much more serious. I made an error of judgment. I refused to accept the fact, could not accept the fact, that for once in my life I failed. I couldn't admit that failure and that was a tragic mistake.[1]

Madoff didn't set out to mastermind the grandest Ponzi scheme in history. He got there one step at a time.

Business guru Jim Collins wrote about this type of ethical truth after studying business executives who've somehow gone wrong. He said:

If you told them 10 years ahead of time, 'Hey, let's cook the books and all get rich,' they would never go along with it. But that's rarely how people get drawn into activities that they later regret. When you are at step A, it feels inconceivable to jump all the way to step Z, if step Z involves something that is a total breach of your values. But if you go from step A to step B, then step B to step C, then step C to step D … then someday, you wake up and discover that you are at step Y, and the move to step Z comes about that much easier.[2]

And denial will keep you telling yourself there's no problem.

# King of Denial

That's the way it happened for King David. You know the story (2 Sam. 11–12). David was at the top of his game, enjoying great success as king for his country. But David made some devastating mistakes; then, instead of confessing his secret sins, David chose to cover them up.

It began one night on the high roof of his palace. It was the custom of the day for women to bathe on their rooftops at certain hours of the night with ceremonial water that had been naturally gathered. And the water on the roof would be kept warm by the sun.

Did David know what he would see when he stepped out onto that roof?

Perhaps this was David's version of flipping through pay-per-view channels. On this particular night, he saw a woman bathing and told his servant, "Find out who this woman is for me."

The servant, however, already knew the answer. He replied, "She is Bathsheba … the *wife* of Uriah the Hittite" (2 Sam. 11:3). In other words, "David, the woman you're lusting over is the wife of one of your most trusted soldiers, who is fighting on the battlefield right now."

As I read about this rooftop moment, it seems to me that God was waving a big red flag for David. He used a servant to try to get David's attention. David ignored the warning, invited Bathsheba to the palace, and had an affair with her.

Then came Bathsheba's three-word note: "I am pregnant." This should have been an awakening moment that would bring David to a place of brutal honesty. It was time to come clean and confess. But David was in denial.

He started scheming. First he brought Bathsheba's husband back from the battlefield, hoping the soldier would sleep with his wife and assume the baby was his own. It didn't work.

So David tried again. He got Uriah drunk and sent him home, hoping this time he would sleep with his wife. It still didn't work. David's options for covering up the situation became fewer and more desperate.

David found himself at step Y. Instead of choosing honesty, he chose more cover-up. He wrote a letter instructing his commander Joab to put Uriah on the front lines of the fiercest fighting, then to pull back and let him be killed.

It worked. Uriah was killed in battle, and David thought maybe this was now over. Now he could move on and no one else had to know what he'd done.

Sometimes, we wish that's how life worked, don't we?

If only ignoring the problem would make it go away. But many of us have learned that an unopened credit-card bill doesn't stave off problems. Instead, every day of denial only increases the balance, which will eventually have to be paid. Denial leads farther down a path than you ever imagined you would go.

## *My AHA*

Think of a time when you dug yourself into a problem much deeper by choosing denial and cover-up. What did you learn from the experience?

_____

_____

_____

_____

_____

_____

Are you choosing denial now? What is your current opportunity to choose honesty before your problem snowballs?

# DAY 19

## *Tricks We Use*

*If we claim to be without sin, we deceive*
*ourselves and the truth is not in us.*

1 John 1:8

I was getting dressed one Sunday morning to go to church when my wife said, "Are you going to preach in that shirt?" which translates, "You're not going to preach in that shirt—are you?"

"Well, yeah," I said. "Do you not like it?"

"No, I like it fine, but did you know it's pink?" she asked.

Now, my wife has nothing against guys in pink, but in sixteen years of marriage she'd never seen me in a pink shirt.

"No, it's not," I said. "This is not a pink shirt. It's light red."

My wife smiled and said, "Light red *is* pink."

"No, no it's not," I said. "I feel confident. I even saw the shirt in the store and thought, *That's a red shirt, but not too red. I like that.*"

But I had to confess it's not too red—because it's a pink shirt.

My eyes communicated, *Hey, it's light red; it's not pink. It's fine.* And even once I found out it was pink, I said, "Well, pink is the new black, right?"

# Three Tactics of Denial

We go to great lengths to tell ourselves something other than the truth, to keep an illusion going rather than get honest with our reality. We're willing to use all sorts of methods to justify our choices and actions and to turn off the alarms of awakening. Denial is a powerful tool, and it comes in several forms.

## 1. Disagree

You've probably had a conversation with someone who was blatantly wrong, but who still kept disagreeing. This disagreement has less to do with the facts and more to do with what he or she wants to be true. It's the old adage, "Don't bother me with the facts; my mind's already made up." We're willing to lie to ourselves about our reality and about what we believe if it means we can have something we want.

I ran into a young man who had grown up in my church and was home on college break. He wanted to talk and explain to me all the reasons he had concluded that sex before marriage isn't a sin. He argued that scriptures about the oneness God had in mind for marriage don't apply anymore.

I said, "My guess is that you've gotten yourself a girlfriend … and you're sleeping with her. Is that true?"

Silence.

Finally he said, "Yeah, but that doesn't have anything to do with this."

We tell ourselves a lie, because the lie is more convenient to believe.

## 2. Defend

Defensiveness often reveals an area of our lives where we're in denial. We point the finger back at someone else or we avoid the people and places that force us to be brutally honest. I've discovered that this is often why people have significant lapses in church attendance. I'll talk to people who come back to church after being away from it for a period of months or years, and they'll usually say something like:

"When I went to college, I started partying, and I guess that was about the time I stopped going to church ..."

"I started dating this guy, and it wasn't long after that I stopped going to church ..."

"My marriage was falling apart, and it was about the same time I filed for divorce that I stopped coming to church ..."

I'm not even sure they realize the connection they are making. They avoided the people and places that might confront them with the truth about where they were.

## 3. Distract

It's easy for us to live in denial about one part of our life if the other parts are keeping us busy and going well.

It's the workaholic who gets a job promotion and is awarded Salesman of the Year, but he's completely oblivious to the fact that his teenage son is smoking pot and his wife feels completely alone.

It's the mother who keeps a beautiful home by constantly decorating and cleaning, but doesn't seem to notice that her children just go to their rooms and shut their doors.

It's the twentysomething who knows every TV-show reference, but fails to take notice that all his friendships are becoming more and more shallow, no longer based on things that actually matter.

But simply choosing to not look at the cancer eating away at our lives doesn't keep it from silently metastasizing until it's terminal.

Confession is the moment of brutal honesty when we tell ourselves the truth—even when it's not what we want to hear. There are a number of ways the word *confession* can be understood and defined, but here's one definition of confession: to agree. You come to a place where you stop disagreeing with truth and you honestly say, "Here I am."

To pursue AHA, replace disagreement, defensiveness, and distraction with confession.

## My AHA

What is the state of your life, your spirit, your marriage—as it truly, actually is? Write it briefly on the following page. Then read it back and circle any hints of denial—or points that prick you because you know you've written them with a "yeah, but …" motivation. Want to get fully and brutally honest? Read your story to your spouse or closest friend or mentor, asking him or her to flag any hints of denial of reality.

_____

_____

_____

_____

_____

_____

# DAY 20

## Confession Is the Cure

*Wash me clean from my guilt. Purify me from my sin.*
Psalm 51:2 NLT

King David lived in denial for a year after his initial sin with Bathsheba. On the outside, things still looked good. He reigned successfully, penning psalms and winning wars, but he had yet to truly acknowledge his sin. He'd tucked it away, fenced it off. He hadn't been honest and hadn't been broken over it. God had given him time, but he still hadn't confessed. So God sent the prophet Nathan to make things clear for David. You can read about this confrontation in 2 Samuel 12.

"David, a situation has come up," Nathan told the king. "There are two men in your kingdom. One man is wealthy and has all kinds of sheep, a great herd. But his neighbor is poor and has only one lamb. This lamb is like a child to the poor man, because he has nothing else. The lamb eats the food off his table and sleeps at the foot of his bed. But, David, here's what happened: The rich man, the one with all the sheep, had a friend over, and they decided that for dinner, they really wanted a rack of lamb. Instead of killing one of his own sheep, the rich man went over to his poor neighbor's house and took that lamb. He stole it, barbequed it, and served it to his friend. What should we do here, David?"

David was furious. He demanded justice for the poor man and said, "The man who did this deserves to die!" Then Nathan stopped him and said four words:

"You are that man."

After multiple cover-ups and a year of denial, David finally broke. He was finally honest with himself, Nathan, and God.

## The Cure

Confession is the only cure for denial.

Every one of us would prefer to skip this part of AHA. After we have the sudden awakening, we are ready to move on with our lives. But lasting change and true transformation require honest confession. The word for "confession" in the New Testament most commonly means "to acknowledge." You acknowledge the reality of your situation.

Psalm 51 is a record of David's prayer of confession. It may be the most honest confession in the Bible. Through brokenness and tears, David finally tells the truth to himself and to God. He is no longer trying to cover up the truth and pretend that everything is okay. No, he is getting everything out and asking God to wash him clean.

> Have mercy on me, O God,
>> because of your unfailing love.
> Because of your great compassion,
>> blot out the stain of my sins.
> Wash me clean from my guilt.
>> Purify me from my sin.
> For I recognize my rebellion;
>> it haunts me day and night.
> Against you, and you alone, have I sinned;
>> I have done what is evil in your sight.
> You will be proved right in what you say,
>> and your judgment against me is just.
> For I was born a sinner—

yes, from the moment my mother
conceived me.
But you desire honesty from the womb,
teaching me wisdom even there.
Purify me from my sins, and I will be clean;
wash me, and I will be whiter than
snow.
Oh, give me back my joy again;
you have broken me—
now let me rejoice.
Don't keep looking at my sins.
Remove the stain of my guilt.
(Ps. 51:1–9 NLT)

## My AHA

Read Psalm 51 again. But this time, instead of reading David's
words, pray them. Then write your own psalm of confession.

_____

_____

_____

_____

_____

# DAY 21

## *Blame Game*

*I will set out and go back to my father and say to him:*
*Father, I have sinned against heaven and against you.*

Luke 15:18

Trina Thompson was having trouble finding a job after she graduated from Monroe College in 2009. There was a severe recession going on in America at that time. Remember it? Jobs were scarce. Unemployment was sky-high. It wasn't just inexperienced recent graduates struggling to find work; hordes of workforce veterans were out of work too.

So what did Trina do? She blamed her college and sued her alma mater for failing to advance her career.[1]

In Idaho five prison inmates got together and made a discovery. Their crimes were different: manslaughter; grand theft;

aggravated battery, including shooting a man; and drug convictions. But they realized alcohol was a common component
of their crimes and poor decisions.

So was this a common awakening and shared experience of
awakening and honest confession? No, the five inmates were fil-
ing a $1 billion lawsuit against eight large alcohol corporations.
The men claimed they never would have started drinking as
minors if they had known alcohol is addictive. In their opinion,
it was the brewers' fault for not warning them on their bottles.[2]

These are just a few reasons why we have so many warning
signs everywhere we look. Do you know why all these warning
labels exist? Most likely because at some point, someone sued
the company over that particular issue.

How do you explain the labels that come on our coffee
cups that read, "Caution: Coffee May Be Hot." Somebody
probably burned her mouth or spilled hot coffee on herself and
then sued the restaurant. See the stroller warning label that says,
"Warning: Remove infant before folding stroller for storage."
Wow. Some parent[†] absentmindedly folded up his toddler and
sued the company for it. A Batman costume has a warning that
reads, "Warning: Cape does not enable user to fly." First of all,

---

†    ~~parent~~ dad

everyone knows Batman doesn't fly. That's Superman. But some kid must've gotten on the top bunk and launched spread eagle across his bedroom, probably breaking a femur in the process. Mom came running in and said, "Does that costume not have a warning label on it!"

If you don't believe me, look them up.

After finding these online, I couldn't help but notice warnings on items around my house. The worst one I found was in my garage. The label on my chainsaw says: "Do not attempt to stop chain with hands."

Our society has become masterful at blaming others for our own foolish choices. Instead of being brutally honest with ourselves, most of us want to place the blame on others. The word for this is *projection*. Projection is when we admit the reality of an unpleasant fact, but we deny responsibility. Denial is refusing to admit the reality of an unpleasant fact, but projection is admitting that the reality exists without taking responsibility for it. We just blame someone else.

## She Did It

This approach is as old as time. It goes all the way back to Adam and Eve. After the Devil came on the scene and did what he does best—lie—after Eve took a big bite of the fruit, after Adam bit in, God confronted Adam and asked, "Have you eaten from the tree that I commanded you not to eat from?" *Boom*. That's a sudden awakening. So how did Adam respond?

> Yes, God. I confess. I broke Your command. I have sinned and not obeyed Your word. Here and now I take responsibility for my rebellion. I don't deserve it, but I humbly ask You for Your grace and mercy.

Okay, that's not exactly how it went. When God confronted Adam, here's what happened: The man said, "The woman you put here with me—she gave me some fruit from the tree, and I ate it" (Gen. 3:12).

That's projection.

Instead of being honest and confessing his sin, Adam basically said, "God, this isn't my fault. It's her fault."

Projection is when we follow our sudden awakening with excuses and justifications. Instead of accepting responsibility, we assign blame:

> "I know it was wrong to change the numbers, but my boss has unrealistic expectations."

"I know it was wrong to plagiarize my paper, but everyone does it."

"I was wrong to lose my temper, but you should have seen the house I grew up in."

"I was wrong to be disrespectful to my husband, but he is so passive."

"I know it's wrong for me to look at that stuff, but my wife doesn't even try anymore."

Instead of staying in denial or projecting his mistakes on someone else, the Prodigal Son was honest about his reality and said, "Here I am starving to death!" He said, "I have sinned." There is something beautiful about that short phrase. Those three words set him on a path to freedom.

## My AHA

Try this. Say these four words: "I am a sinner."

Say it again. This time out loud: "I am a sinner."

Now name your sin without following it with any blame or excuses.

_____

_____

_____

_____

_____

_____

_____

# DAY 22

## *The Usual Suspects*

*Why do you look at the speck of sawdust in your
brother's eye and pay no attention to the plank in your
own eye? How can you say to your brother, "Let me
take the speck out of your eye," when all the time there
is a plank in your own eye? You hypocrite, first take
the plank out of your own eye, and then you will see
clearly to remove the speck from your brother's eye.*

Matthew 7:3–5

A few years ago, I pulled into a crowded parking lot. After
circling enough laps to complete a NASCAR race, I finally
found what may or may not have been a compact-car spot.
I squeezed my truck in, sighing with relief. Ominous storm
clouds swirled overhead. The wind was picking up. I needed
to hurry.

As I opened my door, the wind literally took the door out of my hands. I watched my truck door slam into the car next to me, a relatively new-looking Toyota Camry.

I left my insurance information for the owner of the car, thinking I would have to pay for the damages. A few days later, I was on the phone with my insurance agent, explaining how the wind had ripped the door out of my hands. And he said something that shocked me: "Well, this isn't your fault." I told him there was no way it was the other guy's fault because he was in the store at the time.

My agent replied, "No, it's not your fault, because this is what we call an act of God."

I said, "Really, this is God's fault? We can blame Him for this?" And it turns out that *act of God* is a legal term. So instead of taking responsibility for parking too close and not hanging on to the door tight enough, I got to blame God.

And that's what many of us do. If your marriage doesn't meet your expectations; if your child rebels; if you lose your job; if the economy collapses; if there is a famine in the land—we call it an act of God.

# Easy Targets

There are many different people the Prodigal Son could have blamed for the position he found himself in, but he didn't. He could've taken on the role of the victim in all of this and said, "It's not my fault."

He could have blamed his friends. After all, he spent all his money on partying. It's safe to assume he probably blew through his money buying drinks for a group of newly acquired friends. When the money disappeared, they did too.

He could have blamed the pig farmer and complained that he wasn't being treated fairly. Never mind a fair day's wage, the farmer wouldn't even let him satisfy his appetite with the food the pigs were eating.

And don't you think the Prodigal Son could've blamed his dad for being too permissive or too passive? After all, what kind of father just gives his child his inheritance when it's asked for?

Mom and Dad tend to be easy targets for projecting blame. Instead of taking responsibility, many people become bitter and blame their parents for the way they were raised. Sometimes it only seems fair. Parents make mistakes, and some parents irresponsibly leave lasting scars on their children.

However, I have begun to listen for this kind of projection when I talk to people who need to make a change in their lives. I listened to a single mom in her midthirties who had no trouble being honest about her reality. She had been in and out of relationships her whole life. The longest she ever held the same job was eighteen months. She admitted to treating her depression by shopping. Consequently, she'd racked up all kinds of credit-card debt. But in the first two minutes of the conversation, she told me, "What am I supposed to do? I can't change my childhood, can I?" After defining reality for five minutes, she spent about fifteen blaming her parents.

It wasn't hard to sympathize with her. The truth is, her parents did a lot of things wrong and deeply wounded her when she was young and vulnerable.

But did her parents rack up the credit-card debt? Did her parents make her quit a dozen jobs? Did her parents tell her who to date? Instead of being honest with herself, she was stuck in the pigpen of projection.

There's a difference between being honest about our pain and being honest about our responsibility. As long as we continue to say, "It's not my fault," and blame our parents, God, spouses, bosses, exes, friends, or anything else, true AHA won't happen.

We can't change our past, but when we're willing to take responsibility and come to God honestly in AHA, He can change our future.

## My AHA

Draw a circle. Inside it, write down all the problems and challenges you are having—in life, in your marriage, in your job, with God, whatever. Then draw lines to carve out the piece of the pie that represents your responsibilities for the problems and challenges. Choose to forgive those in the other slices.

# DAY 23

## *It Is a Big Deal*

*Jesus replied, "Very truly I tell you, everyone
who sins is a slave to sin."*

John 8:34

I was sitting in a coffee shop with my MacBook open on the table in front of me. I was working on my sermon for the upcoming weekend. I was just wrapping it up when an older gentleman from the church came over, set his coffee cup on the table, extended his hand, and introduced himself to me. As he began talking, he accidentally knocked over his coffee, which spilled right onto my computer keyboard. I watched in horror as twenty ounces of fresh coffee soaked my computer. The screen almost immediately flashed and shut off.

When I looked at the man, it was clear he didn't realize what he had done. He chuckled and said, "Oh, sorry

about that." Then he tottered off to grab a fistful of nap-
kins before returning to dab the keyboard, sopping up the
coffee.

Meanwhile, I was in shock. Everything was in slow
motion. It became an out-of-body experience. I kept thinking,
*Is this really happening?* Still on napkin duty, the old man tried
to lighten the mood. He pointed to the Apple logo on my Mac
and said, "Looks like someone already took a bite out of that
apple anyway."

He had a good laugh at that one.

I grabbed my computer, shut it, and practically ran away. I
didn't even know where I was going. I could feel the hot coffee
coming out of my computer. I was thinking of everything on
my hard drive that still needed to be backed up. Including my
sermon for that weekend.

A few days later he called my office to apologize, and
then he said, "I hope your computer dried out, and it didn't
end up being a big deal." I didn't have the heart to tell him
the truth.

He still jokes with me about it every now and then,
because to him it was just a small accident.

That's minimization—though in this case, it was
unintentional.

# Maximum Grace

*Denial* is refusing to acknowledge the reality of a situation. *Projection* is acknowledging the reality of the situation but denying any responsibility. *Minimization* is acknowledging the reality of the situation and even owning responsibility for it but denying its seriousness.

Minimization is another tactic we use to avoid honesty. We tell ourselves partial and palatable truths. We downplay and tell ourselves, "It's not that bad."

It took a while for the Prodigal Son to tell himself the truth. He may have minimized along the way before he finally told himself the truth: "Here I am starving to death!" He finally acknowledged just how desperate his situation was. And in his moment of brutal honesty, he practiced the speech he would give his father upon returning home. There was no downplaying involved. In Luke 15:18–19, he told the truth about where his sin and rebellion had led: "Father, I have sinned against heaven and against you. I am no longer worthy to be called your son; make me like one of your hired servants."

I'm not sure who first said it, but there's an old saying that goes likes this:

*Sin will always take you farther than*
*you want to go.*
*Sin will always cost you more than*
*you want to pay.*
*Sin will always keep you longer than*
*you want to stay.*

Scripture doesn't minimize the consequences of sin. We repeatedly see just how seriously God takes it.

In the Old Testament, when God wanted to warn the people that destruction was coming, He would most often send a prophet. The prophet would confront the people with the truth of where things were heading. The people would frequently minimize the prophet's message. Instead of repenting and turning back to God, they would continue down the same path and reap the consequences of their sin. When they ignored God's messages through Jeremiah, for example, Israel was enslaved by the Babylonians for seventy years.

But when the people were brutally honest and repented of their sin, God would respond with compassion and grace. The prophet Joel told Israel,

Return to the LORD your God,

for he is gracious and compassionate,

slow to anger and abounding in love,

and he relents from sending calamity.

(Joel 2:13)

God's offer of compassion and grace is still wide open to us. It's the whole point of the story of the Prodigal Son. He waits with open arms for us to awaken, get honest, and take action to return to Him. Being honest about our sin means we stop minimizing and instead recognize that whatever took us to the Distant Country is a big deal, after all.

Thankfully, our heavenly Father's love and forgiveness are a much bigger deal.

## My AHA

In what specific areas of your life do you find yourself saying, "It's just …" or "It's only …"?

_____

_____

_____

_____

What has become a habit that you can't quit on your own?

_____

_____

_____

_____

# DAY 24

## Excuses, Excuses

*When he comes, he will prove the world to be in the wrong about sin and righteousness and judgment.*

John 16:8

There is a book titled *Over the Edge: Death in Grand Canyon.* As you might guess, it's not a real uplifting read. The author chronicles the nearly seven hundred deaths that have taken place at the Grand Canyon since the 1870s. What was surprising to me was not *that* so many people had died there but *how* many of the deaths occurred. A number of people have fallen to their deaths simply because they were joking around.

In 1992 a thirty-eight-year-old father was teasing his teenage daughter and pretended to lose his balance and fall, laughing at the gag. One second he was pranking his daughter, and then suddenly the fake fall became very real. He stumbled a bit too far and fell four hundred feet to his death.

More recently, in 2012, an eighteen-year-old woman was hiking around the North Rim with friends and thought it would be fun to have her picture taken next to the edge where there was a sign that read, "Stay Away." Just an ironic picture for Facebook to show she was a true adventurer. As she clambered to where the sign stood, several rocks gave way beneath her, and she fell 1,500 feet.

As a pastor, I've discovered that people often blow off warnings by minimizing consequences. In their minds, they are just having fun. But what we don't realize is that it's all leading somewhere. The Prodigal Son was living it up in the Distant Country, but he was closer to the edge than he realized, and eventually the rocks gave way. They always do.

In tears a woman told me how, because of an affair, she lost everything: her marriage, family, and relationship with her kids. With tears running down her cheeks, she shook her head and said to me, "It just started with some harmless flirting at work."

The journey to the pigpen almost always starts when we minimize our sin.

# Things Will Get Better

"Things will get better," we tell ourselves in another way to minimize our sin and its consequences. I'm sure the Prodigal Son told himself this multiple times: when he ran low on money, when his food supply dwindled, when he couldn't find a decent job, or maybe on his first day in the pigpen.

I have a friend who has struggled with a gambling addiction for a long time. It began as just a fun distraction. He would bet twenty bucks on a game now and then. Then one weekend he went with some buddies to Vegas and started playing the slot machines. He got down a few hundred dollars but kept telling himself, "Things will get better." By 4:00 a.m. he had lost more than $7,000 and drained his checking account. When he came home, he couldn't bring himself to tell his wife what happened. Besides, he was sure his luck would change, because things couldn't get much worse, right? He started spending more and more time at the horse races, which are popular here in Kentucky.

Fast-forward three years. He has maxed out thirteen credit cards. His gambling debts are in the millions. He has been fired for suspected embezzlement. His wife has moved out. His house is in foreclosure. But do you know what he said to me last time we talked? He said, "My luck is going to change; I can feel it." In other words, "Things will get better."

I can't help but wonder:

*What's it gonna take?*

*What's it gonna take for you to realize how bad things have gotten?*

*What's it gonna take to move away from the edge?*

*What's it gonna take for you to admit that your marriage has fallen apart?*

*What's it gonna take for you to get some help for your addiction?*

*What's it gonna take for you to realize you're losing your kids?*

*What's it gonna take for you to seek God's help?*

*Seriously, how far does this have to go?*

To experience AHA, you don't need to back away from the edge. You need to turn and run.

## My AHA

Write a step you can take today to turn and run from sin.

_____

_____

_____

# DAY 25

## *This Time It Is a Big Deal*

*I have hidden your word in my heart that*
*I might not sin against you.*

Psalm 119:11

I was back in my hometown of Joplin, Missouri, after the mile-wide EF5 tornado obliterated much of the town in 2011. I visited with a friend who had lost his home. Everything was gone. The only reason his wife and children survived is because they took shelter in a crawl space.

"Do you usually go down there when the sirens sound?" I asked.

"No, not usually," they answered.

"Why did you go this time?" I asked.

"This time it was different," they said.

I didn't think much of it until later that afternoon. I was talking to another friend whose house was completely destroyed. He's usually a laid-back, easygoing guy, but in the storm he had taken his family down the street to a neighbor's house where they had a basement.

"Do you usually do that?" I asked.

You see, when I grew up there, tornado sirens were a pretty common sound. They would go off, but we wouldn't always do anything about it.

"No, not usually," my friend replied.

"Then why did you go?" I asked.

"This time it was different," he said.

For some of you, this time needs to be different.

God is sounding an alarm. Sirens have gone off. You know that you need to get up. But you're still denying or minimizing or blaming other people. Instead of getting up and going to safety while a devastating monster of a storm approaches, you're still saying, "It's not that big of a deal."

## Seeing a Different Standard

That's probably what the Prodigal Son would have said if someone had tried to warn him about where his decisions were leading. In fact, "It's not that big of a deal" is a phrase I often hear when confronting someone about the choices he or she is making.

The problem is we don't realize how bad things are. When you spend too much time in the Distant Country, you start to compare yourself to the people around you, saying, "If everyone is living this way, then what's the big deal?" It's the slippery slope of the Distant Country. Soon your perspective becomes warped. After spending enough time in the Distant Country, you feel like the sin and rebellion are not a big deal because everyone is doing it. And when everyone is doing it, it's harder to be brutally honest about your own condition.

I saw it happen about ten years ago when we moved into a neighborhood in which no one took great care of their lawns. We all mowed when we got around to it. No one fertilized or specially treated their grass. There were a lot of weeds. We seemed to have an unspoken agreement that dandelions were actually beautiful flowers, and the more you had, the prettier your yard looked. We were all quite content and happy living this way. Then one day a new neighbor moved in next door. We'll call him Jonah. Anyway, Jonah began to take meticulous care of his grass. Have you ever had a neighbor like that? They use dark magic to give their lawn some checked pattern.

Think it sounds great to have a neighbor with a beautiful lawn? It was annoying. Jonah's yard revealed the truth about our yard. His commitment to excellence was an indictment against our commitment to mediocrity. And it just took the one neighbor coming in and holding up a different standard for the rest of us to be more honest about what a mess things had become.

In large part, this was the purpose for Old Testament Law. God revealed His perfect standard to us, and we realized just how bad things are. God's Word is meant to get our attention so we won't minimize our sin, but rather realize the seriousness of the situation. When we fill our hearts and minds with Scripture, God uses it to direct and guide us, to sound the alarm when necessary, and to realign our perspectives to His own regardless of the neighbors around us.

God's Word should get our attention and help us see that some things are a bigger deal than we previously realized. But too often we don't take God's Word seriously. Too often we minimize the Word of the Lord. Maybe because of its familiarity. "Familiarity breeds contempt," the saying goes. But it may be more accurate to say that "familiarity breeds indifference." The more we hear some warnings, the less seriously we take them—like those tornado warnings when I was a kid.

It's time to seek God's Word and pay attention. It's time for us to listen and say, "This time it's different."

## My AHA

What is God saying to you through His Word? Ask Him to speak to you as you read the Bible. Start with Psalm 119:9–16.

# DAY 26

## *Settling the Bill*

*For the wages of sin is death, but the gift of God*
*is eternal life in Christ Jesus our Lord.*
Romans 6:23

God sent Jonah to Nineveh to warn the people of coming destruction. You know the story about what a roundabout way Jonah took. But eventually Jonah reached the city and delivered this message from God in Jonah 3:4: "Forty more days and Nineveh will be overthrown."

It might be the shortest sermon in the history of the world. It's only eight words long. Actually it's only six words long in the original Hebrew. Jonah showed up and started preaching that in forty days the city would be destroyed.

Jonah didn't downplay the message. He didn't open up with a joke to ease the tension. He didn't apologize for hurting their feelings. He didn't minimize sin or its coming consequences. Jonah's message was direct and straightforward: "You've got a little more than a month, and then it's lights out for you, Nineveh." Apparently it was enough. The next three words changed everything for Nineveh. We read simply: "The Ninevites believed."

They didn't minimize the situation. They didn't say, "Oh, Jonah's exaggerating to get our attention. I'm sure it won't be that bad." They didn't say, "Forty days? That's plenty of time. I'm sure things will get better." Instead the people believed. It was hard to hear, but they embraced Jonah's brutal honesty. In fact, they proclaimed a fast for everyone and put on sackcloth.

That's brutal. Sackcloth was an abrasive covering made of goat hair that was worn in public as a sign of repentance and grieving. Does that sound like something a respectable person would wear? Is that something you would do?

Picture Donald Trump publicly fasting. Think of Kim Kardashian putting on sackcloth. This was a gesture of humility. All 120,000 people in the great city in Assyria fasted and put on sackcloth, including the king. And he issued the decree that every single person must "call urgently on God" and "give up their evil ways and their violence" (Jon. 3:8).

The Ninevites did not take God's message lightly. And Jonah 3:10 tells us that when God saw how they turned from their wicked ways, He did not bring upon them the destruction He had threatened.

The people of Nineveh were honest with themselves about themselves. They recognized that their sin was a big deal, and they responded to that truth with confession, repentance, and brokenness.

## Counting the Cost

A friend of mine, a pastor at a large church, made some very unfortunate and public mistakes. His choices cost him his job and his family, and he ended up going through a very expensive divorce. As the dust settled from his disastrous fall, he took the time to count the cost—*literally*. He added up every economic asset and material possession he had lost, including the salary from the years he would have stayed in that position. It was well over half a million dollars. Not counting the moral and relational consequences, my buddy realized that even in the most practical sense, his sin had cost him everything. That's brutal honesty, and AHA doesn't happen without it.

So what about you? Add up your bill. What is the true cost of your sin?

Paul told us, "The wages of sin is death" (Rom. 6:23). That's the bill. Our choice to sin has created a barrier between us and God, taken a toll on our relationship with Him that we can't fix, repair, or pay off on our own.

Let's not minimize the situation. We've lived in offense to a holy, righteous God, who reigns in justice. We deserve death for what we've done. Like the Prodigal Son, we've robbed honor from our Father. We have scorned His provision and fled from His house. We have chosen wild living with strangers over a relationship with Him. Like the Prodigal Son, we've told God we'd be better off if He were dead. We've lived in ways that prove our distrust and disbelief in Him. We've chosen a path that leads to starvation and death, so that's what we deserve.

Despite all of this, God offers us a brand-new inheritance—one that has been reclaimed and redeemed by His Son, Jesus Christ, who loved us enough to come to earth and die for our sins. Romans 5:8 says it this way: "But God demonstrates his own love for us in this: While we were still sinners, Christ died for us."

The bill was totaled up, and Christ died to settle it. He gave everything for us. After being crucified, He rose to life again, and He now beckons us home. In the fullness of our sin, God responded with the fullness of His grace through Jesus Christ.

Have you received that grace? Have you accepted His love? Have you responded with your life? It is the ultimate AHA.

## My AHA

What is the spiritual condition of your heart and life? List and total below the emotional, relational, spiritual, or even literal financial cost of your sin and rebellion. Read Romans 10:9–13. Confess your sin to God and receive the gift of Christ's salvation if you have never done so. Then you can write "Paid in Full" across your life's bill.

_____     _____

_____

_____

_____

_____

_____

# DAY 27

## Time to Get Up

*So he got up and went to his father.*

Luke 15:20

After high school graduation, I joined my senior class for a trip to Dallas, Texas. There, for the first time ever, I saw someone bungee jump. At several hundred feet off the ground, this was one of the tallest jumps in the country.

We watched as a guy got ready to make the leap with nothing but a cord strapped to his ankles. He dove headfirst, and it was clear my fellow students were impressed.

In this moment I experienced a phenomenon known as *word vomit*. It's when a thought spews from your mouth before you can stop it. Here's what came out of my mouth: "I'd do that, but I'm not going to spend forty bucks on it."

I was trying to sound cool enough to bungee jump but too cool to actually spend the money. There was a little commotion behind me, and one of the girls in my class pulled out a twenty-dollar bill and said, "Would this help?"

At that point, my back was against the wall. A girl had called my bluff—in front of everyone. I could've said, "Well, I'm not going to spend twenty bucks on it either," but that wouldn't have gone over well. So without stopping to consider the fact that I don't like heights, I took the twenty dollars and got in line.

As the crane lowered, I told myself: *It's not that high.* But once the platform was at ground level and I stepped onboard, I was nervous. The platform rose higher and higher until the crane finally lurched to a halt. I stepped to the edge and made a horrible choice: I looked down.

Overcome with paralyzing fear, I turned to the crane operator and said, "I can't do it. I just can't do it!" But then a thought struck me, and I asked, "Would you just give me a shove?"

Apparently I wasn't the first guy too scared to jump but too embarrassed to ride the platform back down. The worker replied, "Well, we're not legally allowed to push someone off."

Frustrated with his answer, I replied, "Do you have any other ideas for me?"

"Well, sometimes it works if you just close your eyes and fall," he said. Then he added, "Anybody can do that."

*Well, fine,* I thought, mustering some courage. *That sounds all right. I can do that. I can fall.*

So I stepped to the edge, closed my eyes, and I'm proud to say that … well, I didn't exactly bungee jump; I bungee *fell.*

# Beyond Intentions

It's one thing to say what you are going to do, but it's another thing to do it. Action is where a lot of us get stuck. We know what needs to be done, but when we step out onto the platform, we just can't move.

Maybe this is a helpful picture: Think of AHA as a door that swings on three hinges. The first hinge is *a sudden awakening.* The second hinge is *brutal honesty.* The third and final hinge is *immediate action.* In Luke 15:20 we read a simple phrase that changed the story of the Prodigal Son. Jesus simply said, "So he got up."

The Prodigal Son took immediate action. He recognized that it was time to get up. It was time to do something.

And unless our story also reads, "So he got up," or "So she got up," then nothing really changes. This is where AHA stalls out for so many of us. We have an awakening moment, we even find the strength to be brutally honest, but we never get around to actually doing anything different. We spend much of our lives stuck between honesty and action.

But I want you to see a connection in the story of the Prodigal Son between these two phrases in Luke 15:

> "He came to his senses." (v. 17)
> "So he got up." (v. 20)

Without verse 20, verse 17 doesn't really matter.

Without action, AHA doesn't happen.

My question for you is: When are you going to get up?

## My AHA

Make a list of your recent good intentions, things about which you might have said, "I should …" or "I need to …" Better yet, dig out your list of New Year's resolutions. Where are you stuck? Identify what's holding you back. Get up and overcome an obstacle today.

_____

_____

_____

_____

_____

_____

# DAY 28

## *Change or Die*

*Dear children, let us not love with words or*
*speech but with actions and in truth.*

1 John 3:18

I recently read an article that began with the following paragraph:

> Change or Die. What if you were given that choice? … What if a well-informed, trusted authority figure said you had to make difficult and enduring changes in the way you think and act? If you didn't, your time would end soon—a lot sooner than it had to. Could you change when change really mattered? When it mattered most?[1]

According to the article, the odds are nine to one against you changing—even in the face of certain death. The author based that statistic on a well-known study by Dr. Edward Miller, former CEO of the hospital at, and former dean of, the medical school at Johns Hopkins University. Dr. Miller studied patients whose heart disease was so severe they had to undergo bypass surgery—a traumatic and expensive procedure that can cost more than $100,000 if complications arise. About 600,000 people have bypasses every year in the United States, and 1.3 million heart patients have angioplasties. These procedures provide a real chance for change for the patients. Because of the surgeries, they can now, through lifestyle changes, stave off pain and even death, if they're willing to act on the opportunity.

But they don't, says Dr. Miller's research:

> If you look at people after coronary-artery bypass grafting two years later, 90% of them have not changed their lifestyle. And that's been studied over and over and over again. And so we're missing some link in there. Even though they know they have a very bad disease and they know they should change their lifestyle, for whatever reason, they can't.

In our lives, if a sudden awakening calls attention to our heart disease, I hope we realize something is wrong. Following that, we have to allow brutal honesty to do its work in our hearts—essentially bypassing the lies we've believed or told ourselves. Then we, like the heart patients, have an opportunity to act.

Put another way, awakening happens to us, honesty happens in us, but nothing really changes unless action comes out of us.

## Confusing Feelings for Action

So what keeps us from taking action?

Sometimes we get stuck between honesty and action because we trick ourselves into believing that because we *feel* different, we're actually *doing* something different—even if we haven't done anything yet. We mistake our conviction for real change. So we live with good intentions and strong convictions, but we never actually get around to leaving the pigpen.

Conviction is always an invitation to action. However, when convicted hearts don't lead to changed lives, there are some consistent side effects.

These side effects can also serve as symptoms or warnings that action needs to be taken. See if you recognize any of these symptoms in your life.

## An underlying sense of fatigue and frustration

When you don't take action that aligns your life with your heart, your life begins to violate your heart. And when actions violate convictions, a general sense of fatigue and frustration begins to mark one's life.

It's exhausting trying to live in a way that violates your heart. It leaves you constantly drained. Even secular health experts agree that we generally feel worse when our actions don't line up with our beliefs and values. The American Heart Association says to relieve stress: "Examine your values and live by them. The more your actions reflect your beliefs, the better you will feel."[2]

## Unidentified tension in significant relationships

When you know what you need to do but have yet to do anything, it's only a matter of time before your frustration with yourself spills over onto others. If your life isn't aligned with your convictions, you become a hard person to live with.

Typically this shows up as a critical spirit. Sometimes this shows up in relationships when a person gets overly defensive or treats people with a "what's that supposed to mean?" attitude. People who feel guilty because they haven't taken action in areas of conviction tend to be overly sensitive and defensive, especially about things related to those areas of conviction where they have yet to take action.

## Undirected anger

An awakening without action always leads to guilt. You feel guilty that you aren't living your life in a way that is consistent with your convictions. And guilt almost always surfaces in anger.

I've talked with people who say they struggle with a general sense of anger. It's not that they're angry toward a certain person or about a specific situation; they just feel angry. They try to dismiss it. They say, "Well, that's just the way I am ... I'm just wired that way."

If that describes you at all, is it possible that the reason you can't identify why you're upset is because you're actually angry with yourself? Perhaps you feel guilty because you've been awakened to something but haven't done anything about it.

Getting up and taking action is the solution for over-coming any of these obstacles—and for experiencing the full power of AHA.

## My AHA

Rate your levels of each of the following in a scale of one to ten:

Underlying sense of fatigue and frustration:

_____

_____

Unidentified tension in significant relationships:

_____

_____

Undirected anger:

_____

_____

Now add an action step by each category to follow up and do.

# DAY 29

## Changing Your Story

*I will give you a new heart and put a new spirit in you; I will remove from you your heart of stone and give you a heart of flesh.*

Ezekiel 36:26

I read an article about a little boy in a toy store.[1] He was a two-and-half-year-old, so excited to look around aisles stacked with playthings. But it was October, and he didn't see the Frankenstein until he turned around and was face-to-face with the creepy green monster.

This poor little toddler was so terrified that he ran wailing deep into the store and had to be carried out with his face hidden in his mother's arms. He couldn't bear to even look again at the frightening creature.

The image haunted him for hours. His mother tried to talk him through the scary experience, but he kept bringing it back up. It was like a video looping again and again in his mind, and he couldn't get past it.

Then suddenly after recounting the event again, he exclaimed, "I peed on him!"

And with that he triumphed over Frankenstein and his fear.

What the young boy had unknowingly discovered was what psychologists call story editing. Timothy Wilson, a professor of psychology at the University of Virginia, wrote a book about the process called "Redirect." In it, he describes the power of story editing as a tool for emotional healing from painful or difficult events in the past. He encountered the method in a study to help struggling college students improve their academic success after shifting their story from "I'm bad at school" to "Everyone fails at first." And he claims to have seen it work for firefighters processing traumatic experiences on the job.[2]

Essentially the process is editing your life story; it is taking action to change it.

In order to experience AHA, we must change our stories through action.

# Not Easy, but Simple

If the Prodigal Son had come to his senses but had never gotten up, then the story wouldn't have changed. If you've been stuck between coming to your senses and actually getting up, it's time to get up.

I talked to a man who told me his wife had just left him. For the first time he's clearly seeing some things he hadn't seen before. In the past he'd been proud and defensive and had blamed her for everything. Now he realized that he'd put his work first, and he'd been putting his own needs ahead of hers and acting selfishly and pridefully.

When she left him, it was an awakening in his life that forced him to be honest and repentant.

Here's the question I asked him: "Okay, so what's the plan?"

"No, you don't understand," he said. "It's … umm … well, it's complicated."

"No, you don't understand," I replied. "It may not be easy, but it's simple."

It's not easy to get up. I get that. But it is simple. Sometimes we have this complicated mess, and we want to address the complicated mess with a complicated plan, but really the truth is as simple as, "So he got up." Again, I'm not saying it's easy. The journey home would have been difficult. It would not have been easy to make that journey from the Distant Country on an empty stomach, but he got up and went.

So I know the journey won't be easy for this husband, but I am praying that the next part of his story reads, "So he got up."

# When ...?

My question for you is: When are you going to get up?

When are you going to say to a friend, "Look, I've been able to keep it a secret, but I have a drinking problem, and I need help because things are starting to spin out of control."

When are you going to end the relationship that you know God wants you to end?

When are you going to be generous the way you know God has called you to be generous?

When are you going to makes amends with the parents you've wounded?

When are you going to join a Bible study group for the first time in your life?

When are you going to start spiritually leading your family?

When are you going to talk to one of your coworkers about your faith?

When are you going to do something real about the social justice causes you post about online?

When are you going to invite your neighbor to church?

When is verse 20 going to be a part of your story?

*It's time to get up.*

## My AHA

Edit your story. Pick a painful or difficult experience— probably one connected to an awakening. For each of the next three or four days, spend fifteen minutes writing about it. Write honestly and explore your emotions freely. Explore how you would like to see God use this experience to shape you.

# DAY 30

## Getting Past Passivity

*But you will receive power when the Holy
Spirit comes on you; and you will be my
witnesses in Jerusalem, and in all Judea and
Samaria, and to the ends of the earth.*

Acts 1:8

Imagine you're on a Hollywood set. The Academy Award winning director has positioned the cast just so. Cameras surround the scene on long, swinging booms. Light towers are angled just right. There's a multimillion-dollar budget to ensure the highest quality production and an ensemble cast filled with A-list actors. They're at the peak of their craft, fully immersed in their characters, ready to deliver another moving performance. The second assistant camera raises the clapboard, opens it, and ... nothing happens.

Until he clacks the board and shouts "Action!" nothing happens. The cameras don't roll. The scene doesn't get shot. The movie isn't made. The story isn't told.

Without action, the finest actors and filmmakers in the world can't make a movie.

Without action, there can't be AHA.

# Action Spectators

It's an interesting irony about us as a society—we love action, but we would rather watch it than live it. We'll sit on the couch and order a pizza while we watch gourmet-cooking shows. We'll watch a home-improvement network for hours, and then get ourselves a drink from a leaky faucet. We will watch the contestants on *The Biggest Loser* push themselves until they are completely exhausted, but when it's over, we don't want to get out of the La-Z-Boy to get the remote control sitting across the room.

We men especially love action movies. Try this, guys: How many movies have you seen in the last six months? How many of them were action movies? Uh-huh. We find inspiration in the fighter who refuses to quit, the embattled soldier who rushes the enemy, or the athlete who rallies the team against all odds.

We've all got our favorites. Of course, everybody knows *Braveheart* and *Gladiator* are the greatest ever. But there are some excellent superhero movies being made now too—although it seems that every superhero and his brother are getting their own movie these days. *Guardians of the Galaxy? Ant-Man?*

Just what is it about superheroes? Is it not enough to be a normal Indiana Jones or Jason Bourne anymore? It seems now we want our heroes to have superpowers. We want to watch them fly or hurl buses and do all the hard work of saving the earth or human civilization.

When we men witness that kind of action, something comes alive in us. When the movie ends, however, what do we do?

Instead of fighting for our wives' honor, we just stand there and let our kids walk all over them.

Instead of being passionate about our marriages, we get passionate about sports.

Instead of fighting against temptation, we tap out and say it's too much.

Instead of getting up, we recline in our La-Z-Boys and flip through our two hundred channels.

What is it that keeps us from acting with a greater sense of urgency? Instead of being aggressive, it seems more natural for us to respond passively. Even when everything is at stake, we kick back on the couch waiting to see what happens, hoping everything will work itself out.

## Ingrained

Passivity could be accurately described as the first sin we inherited from Adam. It may even be fair to say the first human sin wasn't eating the fruit; it was passivity. Remember when Eve took the fruit in the garden of Eden? What was Adam doing? Well, according to Genesis 3:6, Adam was right there with her. She had a conversation with a serpent and Adam just watched.

He said nothing.

He did nothing.

He just stood there.

But look where it got Adam, and contrast him to the Prodigal Son.

The Prodigal Son didn't just hope his luck would change. He didn't wait for the famine to end and the economy to turn around. He came up with a plan of action. He said to himself, "I will set out and go back to my father and say to him ..." (Luke 15:18). That's the opposite of saying, "I will sit down, stay here, and hope for the best."

Once the Prodigal Son had his awakening and got honest with himself, he chose action over passivity.

We must do the same.

We may not have superhero powers, but we have something better. We have the true power of the Holy Spirit alive within us, helping us in our weakness, comforting us, and filling us with His strength.

## My AHA

What are you hoping will work out by itself? It won't. Put aside passivity and take action to work it out. With the Lord's strength, I will ...

_____

_____

_____

# DAY 31

## *Obey Anyway*

*If you love me, keep my commands.*
John 14:15

Read the line below and see if you recognize it:

Up, up, down, down, left, right, left, right,
B, A, start.

Can you identify this code?

It's a cheat code from the Nintendo game *Contra*, which was my favorite game growing up. I am told that it works on several other games as well. I loved *Contra*, but I could never beat it.

One day my friend Brian came over, and we were playing *Contra* when he blew my mind. When the game turned on, he entered that cheat code on the controller—up, up, down,

down, left, right, left, right, B, A, start—and he got thirty free lives. Through some coercion, he gave the cheat to me to use as well, and it changed the way I played. From then on, I didn't even have to try hard. I just assumed everything would work out because I had the cheat code.

Passivity looks for shortcuts, for cheats, for a way around, while immediate action moves directly. Passivity looks for the path of least resistance—the wide path. Immediate action looks for the path of righteousness—the narrow one.

Passivity wants to cheat. Action wants to change.

Passivity says, "Everything will work itself out." Action says, "This is going to take some work."

Passivity says, "What's the least I can get away with?" Action says, "What needs to be done?"

The Prodigal Son finally did the hard thing. He took action. He rejected passivity, made a game plan, and followed through. Action can be that simple and that difficult.

## Obey Anyway

So maybe you see some passivity in your life and know you need to change, but you're thinking, *I agree with you, but I just don't feel like doing anything about it.*

I know how you feel.

It may sound a little cold, or perhaps a bit trite; however, the truth is we need to obey God even when we don't feel like it. When we obey God even without the motivation to do so, our feelings will eventually catch up with our actions.

I remember learning this lesson when we lived in California. One thing that stressed me out there was the traffic. I hated sitting in traffic. One day I was sitting in a line of cars not going anywhere, riding the bumper of the car in front of me. I honked my horn, hoping that somebody miles up the road would hear it and decide to go a little faster. I kept switching lanes, trying to move ahead a few extra feet. I was completely stressed out.

I knew this wasn't what God wanted for me. He wanted me to be at peace. I didn't feel at peace, so I decided to fake it and see what would happen. I thought to myself, *I'm not a man at peace, but if I were, what would I do?*

Well, for starters, I would back off the car in front of me. I would quit honking my horn, and I wouldn't switch lanes. A man at peace would probably put in a sermon or worship CD. So I stuck in a worship CD. A man at peace would probably sing along with this CD, so I started to sing. A man at peace would smile, so I forced myself to smile. A man at peace might wave at somebody, so I waved. I thought a man at peace would probably let someone else in front of him. But it's hard to say for sure, so I didn't go ahead with that one.

I don't know when it happened, but at some point I began to feel at peace. You see, our attitudes and emotions can catch up with our actions. We are called to be obedient even when we don't feel like it. I'm not saying be fake, but I am saying take obedient steps of action even if you don't feel like it at first and let them genuinely align your heart.

Look back at your game plan for the changes you need to make. You've probably made the list before, whether on paper or in your mind; you've listed some in recent chapters in this book. You know what they are. Identify the first step, just like the Prodigal Son did when he pointed out, "I will go home and say to my father …" He knew what he needed to do, and he carried it out. You may find that along the road, with God's help, actions that at first seem artificial can become authentic.

## My AHA

Go ahead. Look at your game plan. Write it down below. What would a man or woman experiencing AHA look like facing a similar situation as you? Circle your first step and act on it now, whether or not you feel like it.

# DAY 32

## *Pick Up Your Sword*

*After I looked things over, I stood up and said
to the nobles, the officials and the rest of the
people, "Don't be afraid of them. Remember
the Lord, who is great and awesome, and
fight for your families, your sons and your
daughters, your wives and your homes."*

Nehemiah 4:14

When it comes to contrasting national leaders, Great Britain
had a pair of prime ministers who rank at the top of the list:
Neville Chamberlain and Winston Churchill.

History has not been kind to Chamberlain. His critics
would say he earned every bit of his reputation as the poster
boy of passive appeasement that allowed the Nazis to flourish
leading up to World War II.

Once Adolf Hitler took leadership of Germany in 1933, he wasted little time thumbing his nose at the rest of Europe by rearming Germany and reclaiming German territories. While France, Britain, and the Soviet Union debated what to do about this aggressive tyrant, Hitler did whatever he wanted.

By 1938 Germany invaded Czechoslovakia. Europeans were worried. World War I was fresh in their memories. It had engulfed much of the world and taken warfare to new hellish depths. People were terrified of another catastrophic war like that. So Neville Chamberlain arranged a meeting with Hitler and reached an agreement. Hitler wouldn't go to war against England. Britain and its European allies wouldn't do anything about his recent invasion. The British leader came home triumphantly announcing he had secured "peace for our time."

Of course, a year later Hitler called the treaty a "scrap of paper" and invaded Poland, launching World War II. Soon Germany was sweeping across Europe.

Chamberlain resigned as prime minister, and Winston Churchill took office. Known as the British Bulldog, Churchill famously rallied Britain's courage and inspired the nation's difficult but successful defense of the German onslaught. As a strong and decisive leader, Churchill forged the alliances with the United States and Soviet Union that were eventually able to defeat Hitler and his allies.

As much as Chamberlain's leadership became synonymous with weakness, Churchill's became known as strength, courage, and determination. Churchill was a leader who inspired action in the face of some of the world's greatest evil.

# Bible Leaders Too

The Bible gives us a contrast of active and passive leaders. Eli was a priest and judge of Israel, but 1 Samuel 2:12 tells us that his sons were scoundrels who "had no regard for the LORD," despite the fact they were priests.

Hophni and Phinehas stole money from the offering, ate the sacrifices meant for God, and slept with the women who served outside the sanctuary. They had *no* regard for the Lord.

So Eli probably didn't know what was happening, otherwise he'd have put a stop to it, right? No, Eli was getting reports about exactly what his sons were doing.

Those reports were an awakening moment for Eli. People spoke the truth to him about his sons, and he experienced brutal honesty. But when it was time for Eli to take action, what did he do? Use tough love, remove his sons as priests, and put the fear of the Lord into them, right?

No, Eli pulled a Chamberlain. He talked to them.

He was what Dr. Phil calls a "threatening parent": a parent who says, "Well, next time …" or "If you do that again …" or "This time I mean it …" Eli said a lot of words but took no action.

## What's More Important?

Scripture gives us a clue as to why Eli was so passive. It's easy to miss, but it's significant in understanding why we so often choose passivity over action.

In 1 Samuel 2:29, God asked Eli: "Why do you honor your sons more than me?"

When Eli did nothing about his sons, he chose his sons over God.

Don't miss this: *our passive approach to the action God has called us to take shows that we are honoring something more than Him.*

He convicts you about a dating relationship—but you don't do anything. Why? Because you honor your significant other more than you honor God.

He convicts you about lust—but you don't take any action, and in doing nothing, you honor your desires more than God.

He convicts you about being generous—but you still haven't started to give. Why? Because you honor your money more than you honor God.

He convicts you to be a spiritual leader—but you come home from work and spend the evening watching TV. Why? Because you honor sports more than God.

Passivity reveals that we've chosen something or someone over God.

## Pick Up a Sword

Nehemiah is the Bible's Churchill to Eli's Chamberlain. Nehemiah led God's people in an effort to rebuild the walls of Jerusalem. It was a huge job, and it reached a point where the work seemed to be too much. Enemies harassed the workers, and the opposition seemed too overwhelming. But Nehemiah called the men of Israel to be men of action. He essentially challenged them by asking, "Did you think this was going to be easy? Did you think the wall was going to just build itself?" And then he said to them, "Pick up a sword and fight" (Neh. 4:13–14).

When will you put down the remote control, choose God, and stand up for your family? Put down the cell phone, pick up a sword, and fight for your marriage. Put down the PlayStation controller, put down the 9 iron, put down the iPad, and fight for something.

## My AHA

Put it down—for a day, for a week—whatever it is that's feeding your passivity and holding you back from action. Instead, follow these actions steps you create every time you'd normally be wallowing in passivity.

1. _____

_____

_____

_____

_____

2. _____

_____

_____

_____

_____

3. _____

_____

_____

_____

_____

# DAY 33

## *Little Guy, Big Change*

*But Zacchaeus stood up and said to the Lord, "Look,*
*Lord! Here and now I give half of my possessions*
*to the poor, and if I have cheated anybody out of*
*anything, I will pay back four times the amount."*

Luke 19:8

Remember Zacchaeus? The wee little man? He's the star of one of my favorite AHA stories in Scripture. Luke 19 says, "He was a chief tax collector and was wealthy" (v. 2). And the word used means "extreme wealth." Zacchaeus was in the top 1 percent of the 1 percenters.

He was also really short. It is rare that the Bible gives a physical description, but when it does, I immediately get an image in my mind of who I would cast for that role. I think Joe Pesci would be a good Zacchaeus, right? He's this little guy who has a high, annoying voice and who dresses really well.

So picture short Zacchaeus in this crowd. Elbows were flying near his face as all these rubbernecks jockeyed for a view of Jesus coming through Jericho. Zacchaeus gave up trying to compete with the crowd and climbed up a sycamore tree. That's where he was perched when Jesus arrived.

Here's what Jesus said in Luke 19:5: "Zacchaeus, come down immediately. I must stay at your house today."

Zacchaeus thought this was great, but the people "began to mutter" that Jesus "'has gone to be the guest of a sinner'" (v. 7).

It wasn't that having money is inherently bad. The problem was how Zacchaeus got his money. Being a chief tax collector meant Zacchaeus was basically the Bernie Madoff of his day, running a kind of ancient Ponzi scheme.

This is how it worked: Jewish tax collectors would go out on behalf of the Roman government—the occupying enemy—and they would take money from the Israelites, their own people. They would say, "Taxes this year are $150." And they'd give one hundred dollars to the Romans and pocket fifty dollars for themselves. This is how tax collectors grew wealthy. Each tax collector would then give a percentage of the fifty dollars they'd pocketed to the chief tax collector. That was Zacchaeus. He sinned for a living. It was his job. When someone hoarded money the way Zacchaeus did, people didn't want to have anything to do with him.

So when Jesus came along and said, "I'm gonna come eat at your house," Zacchaeus was thrilled. It was an honor for this rabbi to stop and eat with him. My guess is that Zacchaeus was used to eating well, but he was used to eating alone.

However, something happened during that meal that changed Zacchaeus's heart.

He had accumulated wealth, but he had also been searching; he had been trying to find some kind of satisfaction. Nothing had worked, but when he met Jesus, he said, "This is it! This is what I have been looking for." He had this sudden awakening because of his encounter with Jesus. He realized that what he was looking for wasn't something one can buy.

Zacchaeus also had to face some hard truths. The reality was that he'd turned his back on his own people and he couldn't blame anyone else. Poor people had become even poorer because of his actions. Peasants had skipped meals because of his greed. He had to look at his life honestly and take responsibility for it.

So this is what we read in verse 8:

> Zacchaeus stood up and said to the Lord,
> "Look, Lord! Here and now I give half of my
> possessions to the poor, and if I have cheated
> anybody out of anything, I will pay back four
> times the amount."

In the wake of his startling realization and in the face
of the honest truth, Zacchaeus took action. Can you imagine how this would've been a testimony to the people in the
community?

## Spread the AHA

Earlier, the people were upset that Jesus was going to go eat
with this sinner. What do you think they thought of Jesus after
Zacchaeus came out and announced that he was going to give
away half of his possessions? They would have been amazed!

When our AHA experience finds its fulfillment in
immediate action, Jesus is glorified. When those people saw
Zacchaeus transformed, they knew it could only be because of
Jesus. The same is true in our lives. Our friends have probably

seen us struggle with making wise choices. When we experience AHA and it results in immediate action and life changes, they will recognize that it wasn't by our power or through our determination. It was because of Jesus.

Here's the phrase I want you to pay special attention to in the story of Zacchaeus. In verse 8, just before Zacchaeus announced his plan he said, "*Here and now I give.*"

Here and now.

I'm not gonna wait until later. I'm not gonna wait until I reach a certain level. I'm not going to put this off. But *here and now* I'm going to be generous and pay back those I cheated.

That's your challenge today. Take action immediately. Let it start *here* and *now*.

## My AHA

Here and now I ...

_____

_____

_____

_____

Mark this time and place and moment that Jesus changed your heart. In Joshua 4:20–24, God told the people to set up twelve stones to serve as markers and reminders of when He took them into the Promised Land. Create your own marker to remind you and others of your AHA.

# DAY 34

## *Killing Time*

*Today, if you hear his voice, do not harden
your hearts as you did in the rebellion.*

Hebrews 3:15

Where would procrastinators be without YouTube? One hundred hours of video are uploaded each minute. Over six billion hours of video are watched each month. It's a procrastinator's dream: dancing cats, toddler antics, epic fails, Psy parodies, and Harlem Shakes. I think I just wasted an hour researching this chapter.

While we have an almost endless stream of digital options for procrastinating today, putting off work or tasks or to-do lists is an ancient practice. The ancient Roman poet Ovid wrote, "Don't put off till tomorrow [the cure] you can work today. If you are not ready today, tomorrow you will be less

215

so."[1] Maybe back then, they ran around looking for live cats they could watch dance and sing; I don't know.

But I did read about some creative possibilities recently. When the BBC published an article about procrastination, hundreds of people responded with their tales of putting things off.[2] One man weighed his cat instead of working. Another lost a $10,000 check from a client and never got around to asking for another one. A woman still has the cans of paint she bought to decorate her bathroom—twelve years ago. And another man hadn't read a book he bought ten years ago: *52 Steps to Defeating Procrastination*.

That's the thing about telling yourself, "I'll get to it later." If you tell yourself that enough, the urgency evaporates, and your procrastination has consequences.

The Prodigal Son's action was immediate. The word "so" in the sentence "So he got up …" indicates a quick response. It's best to understand Luke 15:17 and 20 as one movement. It's a continuation. He said, "Here's what I'm going to do …," and then he got up and did it.

After having an awakening and an honest moment, we often get stuck in the pigpen trying to come up with a plan or promising ourselves that—sometime soon—we will take action. But the Bible doesn't say of the Prodigal Son: "The next day he got up …" or "After some time passed …" or "When the weather was good for traveling …" It says, "So he got up." He took action immediately.

# Putting It Off

Procrastination is one of the chief tools Satan uses to prevent AHA from happening in your life. He knows that if you put off taking action long enough, you will soon go back to sleep. And here's why procrastination is so effective: Even though we are still sitting in the pigpen, we feel as though we've done something. It lets us off the hook because we're not saying, "No"; we're just saying, "Not right now." We're not turning the alarm off; we're just hitting the snooze button.

There are a few reasons why we have this proclivity towards procrastination:

### 1. We want to put off the pain.

We put off the workouts, because we don't want sore muscles.

We put off living within our means, because we don't want to cut back on our lifestyle.

We put off the hard conversation, because we don't want awkward tension.

We put off getting help, because we don't want to feel vulnerable.

We put off asking for forgiveness, because we don't want to embarrass ourselves.

The Prodigal Son knew how hard making the trip back home was going to be. He knew it would be painful to see his father's disappointment. He knew how humbling it would be to face his brother's judgment. But waiting wasn't going to make it any easier. In fact, the longer he put off action, the more difficult it would become.

*So he got up.*

### 2. We want to prolong the pleasure.

The truth is that spending money on wild living in the Distant Country sounds fun. Ultimately, it doesn't last and brings much greater pain. But in the moment, it's fun. There's a reason some people sleep around, get hammered on weekends, or experiment with drugs. They experience earthly pleasure.

Even though we know these kinds of choices lead to the pigpen, we still think we have time to enjoy it. Until the famine comes, we tend to put off any action, believing we can live it up a while longer without multiplying our consequences. Unfortunately, the longer we try to prolong the pleasure, the greater the pain will be.

### 3. We want to plan it to perfection.

Notice that the Prodigal Son's plan of action wasn't complicated. Get up, go home, and talk to his father. He didn't plan a pit stop to get cleaned up. He didn't work up a way to make back a little bit of money, so he wasn't going home broke. He didn't complicate the plan with any unnecessary steps.

Keeping it simple can be hard, but when you try to tie up every possible loose end, you end up frustrated and convinced you need to work harder. Sometimes we just need a simple plan of action—even if it's imperfect.

So what action do you need to take? You may be surprised how something as simple as making a phone call, scheduling an appointment, cutting up a credit card, or unfriending a Facebook friend can be a step toward your journey home.

Quit killing time before it kills you spiritually. If you're thinking, *Tomorrow I will …* or *Next week I'm going to …,* that is not the Holy Spirit. The Holy Spirit always says, "Today …"

## *My AHA*

Tell someone what you are getting up and doing. Making your intentions public is a good motivator to follow through. Today I will tell …

_____

_____

_____

# DAY 35

## *Not Too Late*

*Jesus answered him, "Truly I tell you, today*
*you will be with me in paradise."*

Luke 23:43

Blair Ecker shares his prodigal story in his own—and his mother's—words:

> July 21, 2000
> Psalm 51

> *Father,*
> *You desire honesty from my son's heart,*
> *so You can teach him to be wise in his inmost*
> *being. Purify him from his sins, and he will*
> *be clean. Wash him, and he will be whiter*

*than snow. Oh, Father, give him back his joy again. You have broken him; now let him rejoice. Don't keep looking at his sins; remove the stain of his guilt. Create in him a new heart, oh, God. Renew a right spirit within him. Do not banish him from Your presence, and don't take Your Holy Spirit from him. Restore to him again the joy of Your salvation and make him willing to obey You.*

*Amen*

January 17, 2003
   Psalm 57

*Father,*

*Please have mercy on my son. Help him look to You for protection. Hide him beneath the shadow of Your wings until this violent storm is past. Help him cry out to You, God, the most high, the God who will fulfill Your purpose for him. Please send help from heaven to save him, rescuing him from those*

*who are out to get him. Father, please send*
*forth Your unfailing love and faithfulness.*
    *Amen*

I was the prodigal in these prayers. I knew—and am still ashamed of—the worry I caused my mother. After her death from cancer in 2009, I found stacks of prayer journals with my name on them. Those twelve years' worth of journaling are too painful for me to sit down and read through in their entirety, but I know these prayers changed my life. They echo on after my mother's death and continue to impact me.

After spending time in youth ministry, I was recently hired as a senior pastor. Thank you, Mom—and thank You, Jesus!

# Too Far Gone?

Sometimes in the Distant Country, we see the mess we're in, and instead of taking action, we tell ourselves, "It's too late."

*My kids are too old.*
*My marriage is too broken.*
*My friend is too angry.*
*My reputation is too far gone.*
*My debt is too overwhelming.*
*My addiction is too powerful.*
*My life is too messed up.*

Life can reach a point where it feels like things have gone too far. There are too many broken pieces to put back together. I'm sure the Prodigal Son must have felt that way. His life was way past fixing. But eventually, he must have decided he didn't have anything to lose. He had no money left. He had no friends left. He had no more physical strength. He had no options. Sometimes rock bottom is the best place to be, because that's what it takes to experience AHA, though it doesn't have to be.

# Thief on the Cross

If there was ever a man who must have thought it was too late, it was the man crucified next to Jesus. Matthew 27 tells us that there were two criminals crucified on either side of

Jesus. Scripture also says that they both mocked Him and said cruel things to Him. But something happened to one of the two criminals. He experienced AHA as he hung on that cross next to Jesus.

Luke also records what happened:

> One of the criminals on a cross began to shout insults at Jesus: "Aren't you the Christ? Then save yourself and us." But the other criminal stopped him and said, "You should fear God! You are getting the same punishment he is …But this man has done nothing wrong." Then he said, "Jesus, remember me when you come into your kingdom." Jesus said to him, "I tell you the truth, today you will be with me in paradise." (Luke 23:39–43 NCV)

Do you see it? He had a sudden awakening. He saw who Jesus truly was. He was brutally honest as he admitted that he was getting what he deserved for his sin. Then he took action. He both defended Jesus and cried out to Him for help. With his dying breath, he asked God to save him. What made him think it wasn't too late? He was a convicted criminal dying for crimes he committed, and he had no time left to make things right, no chance to offer restitution to his victims.

What did that thief witness that would have made him think it wasn't too late to act? I think it was the prayer that Jesus prayed on the cross. Jesus prayed for the soldiers who crucified Him. He didn't pray for their destruction. He didn't pray for them to be punished. He prayed that God would forgive them.

This thief was going through the same suffering Jesus was and at the hands of the same soldiers. He would have been filled with anger and rage toward those responsible. But Jesus said, "Father, forgive them" (v. 34).

What do you do with that kind of grace? I think it just wrecked that thief. His heart softened in that moment. Who was this man who spoke forgiveness for His own executioners?

*Maybe,* he must have thought, *it's not too late for me, after all.*

## Open Invitation

It's not too late—for you or for a prodigal you love. Your story isn't done. There is still hope. The Father is waiting. His offer of grace and forgiveness hasn't expired. And there's no qualitative calculation about it—there's no *enough* we have to measure up to. We can't out-right our wrongs, and we don't have to.

God is in the business of healing. He rewrites our stories. He transforms the broken into the whole. He turns rebellious prodigals into pastors. He is "the Father of compassion and the God of all comfort, who comforts us in all our troubles, so that we can comfort those in any trouble with the comfort we ourselves receive from God" (2 Cor. 1:3–4).

Take heart. Grasp hope. The kingdom of God is a home we can always return to. And when we do, the ashes can be turned into beauty.

## My AHA

Write about a time or times when you've seen God reach into pain and eventually produce beauty—in your life or in the life of someone you know.

_____

_____

_____

_____

_____

_____

_____

_____

# DAY 36

## *Come Home*

*So he got up and went to his father.*
*But while he was still a long way off, his father saw him*
*and was filled with compassion for him; he ran to his*
*son, threw his arms around him and kissed him.*

Luke 15:20

A friend of mine told me of his AHA story:

> Eight years ago I left home and went to
> Colorado State University. I was in a frater-
> nity, and I majored in partying. For the first
> three semesters, I never stopped and thought
> about what I was doing. I wasn't praying at
> all. After three semesters, reality came crash-
> ing in on me. I could no longer deny what

was happening. I had flunked four of my five classes. It was a wake-up call. I knew I needed to make some changes. I needed to get out of the fraternity and lose some of my friends, but what I really needed was to make a change in my relationship with God—if He would still have me.

In the frat house there was no place with privacy to make the phone call to my parents explaining that I had failed, so I took the phone into the bathroom. I remember there was a stack of pornography, and I didn't want to look in that direction, so I sat on top of it.

I called my parents and explained to them that I had blown it in a lot of areas of my life—not just my grades but also in my walk with Christ. I had strayed from Him. And my parents listened to what I had to say, and then they said three words to me.

They didn't say, "Turn things around."

They didn't say, "Make things right."

They didn't say, "Get some help."

They didn't say, "Figure it out."

They didn't say, "We love you."

They didn't say, "We forgive you."

It was better than that.

What they said to me was: "Just come home."

# The Welcome

As Jesus told the parable of the prodigal son, everyone in the first-century audience was probably thinking the same thing—his father is going to let him have it. The father is going to disown him and will likely refuse to acknowledge his presence. At the very least, that boy was going to be shoveling excrement until he paid his father back—with interest.

The son's action was to get up and go.

But what action would the father take?

It's difficult to tell whether the father was looking, waiting, and hoping for his son to appear on the horizon, or if it was coincidental that he saw him coming from a distance. Perhaps each day he intentionally scanned the horizon. Maybe he happened to glance up from his work and spy his approaching son. As a parent, you know there is hardly a difference. How many days or years had it been for this father? While reality continued to offer no sign of this lost son, he always had hope. Each look outward was underlined with expectancy. Maybe, just maybe, one day …

*Could it be?*

*Was this yet another wishful illusion?*

*Yes. Yes! It … it is … my boy!*

And every cell of this father's being was moving, running, tumbling forward without thought or reason or hesitation. The father did not wait for his son to make it home; he hurried to welcome him. Never had his love wavered.

Here's how Jesus tells it in Luke 15:

> But while he was still a long way off, his father saw him and was filled with compassion for him; he ran to his son, threw his arms around him and kissed him.
>
> The son said to him, "Father, I have sinned against heaven and against you. I am no longer worthy to be called your son."
>
> But the father said to his servants, "Quick! Bring the best robe and put it on him. Put a ring on his finger and sandals on his feet. Bring the fattened calf and kill it.

Let's have a feast and celebrate. For this son
of mine was dead and is alive again; he was
lost and is found." So they began to celebrate.
(vv. 20–24)

# What!

Two parts of this story would have been especially shocking to
first-century listeners. First, when the Prodigal Son asked for
his inheritance from his father while the father was still alive.
It was equivalent to wishing the father were dead.

But even more shocking than the son's blatant disrespect
and coldhearted selfishness is the undeserved grace and extravagant love the father showed when his son returned. The way
Jesus described the grace and love of the father was scandalous.

While the son "was still a long way off," the father ran
to him. Culturally this just didn't happen. The patriarch of a
Jewish family didn't run. He would never hike up his robes
and take off running. It wasn't sophisticated. It wasn't refined.
It wasn't distinguished.

Neither was throwing his arms around him and kissing
him. The father loved the son as he was. He wasn't waiting
for his son to get cleaned up and washed. He gave his sweaty,

stinking, pig-sitting son a big bear hug, and the word for *kissed* here is the image of multiple kisses.

The father wasn't going to wait. Just like God doesn't wait for you to make it home on your own. In fact before you even thought about taking action, He had already acted. The Bible says that while we were still sinners, Christ died for us. While we were still in the Distant Country feeding pig slop to pigs, He acted.

You think, *It's too late now. I don't have time to get cleaned up. I don't have time to get my life together.* But the Father wants you just the way you are.

When you finally act, your heavenly Father comes running with arms wide open. He loves you just as you are, but He doesn't leave you that way. He puts His best robe on your dirty body. He puts the family ring on your hand. He kills the fattened calf and throws an extravagant feast.

## God's Story

The focus of the story quickly shifted from the actions of the son to the actions of the father. You see, Jesus's parable in Luke 15 isn't about a son who rebels. It's about a father who loves his children unconditionally.

In our own lives, we make the story all about us, and it feels like it's too late. But the story is really about the Father. It's about the undeserved, overgenerous, endless love our heavenly Father has for you and me and every prodigal still living in the Distant Country. His invitation always beckons. His hope always remains. His arms are always open. He is waiting to celebrate.

## *My AHA*

What mess are you trying to clean up yourself? What excuses are you still offering?

_____

_____

_____

_____

_____

Write or draw what it feels like to be swept into the Father's embrace.

_____

_____

# DAY 37

## *Older Bro*

*There was a man who had two sons.*

Luke 15:11

When Jesus's audience heard Him tell of the celebration at the son's return to the father, everyone listening assumed the story was over. I imagine Jesus finishing His sentence about the celebration and then pausing. The listeners would have nodded their heads, showing they were intrigued by this interesting story. Everyone likes a happy ending, right? To be fair, "So they began to celebrate" sounds an awful lot like "And they lived happily ever after."

Then Jesus cleared His throat and used a classic transitional word in storytelling. "Meanwhile …," He said.

Attentive listeners might remember that Jesus began the story with a brief but important detail: "A man had two sons."

After that, the story focused completely on the younger son and the father. But when listeners came to the celebration scene, there was no older brother to be found.

That's where we would cut to a split screen if this were a movie. While one side pans a wide-angled horizon with an older man running full tilt toward a plodding traveler, the other side shows a man working the ground tirelessly. While the weeping father smothers his younger son with kisses as he tries to choke out an important message, the older brother tends his father's lands faithfully, with determination. And as the sun sets over the fields and the courtyard fills with guests and food and a beaming father toasts his freshly robed son, the older brother hears a commotion and asks a young servant what's going on.

Now our screen would cut to the older brother as he grows livid listening to the servant's explanation about the return of the younger son and the father's celebration. Invited in by the servant, the older brother turns back to the field in refusal.

Later that evening, the father walks slowly toward his older son in the field, to plead with him to come celebrate the homecoming of his younger brother.

But here's how the older brother responds:

But he answered his father, "Look! All these years I've been slaving for you and never disobeyed your orders. Yet you never gave me even a young goat so I could celebrate with my friends. But when this son of yours who has squandered your property with prostitutes comes home, you kill the fattened calf for him!"

"My son," the father said, "you are always with me, and everything I have is yours. But we had to celebrate and be glad, because this brother of yours was dead and is alive again; he was lost and is found."

Now don't miss this: the older brother never left the father, never broke the rules, never went to a distant country, *but he also never experienced AHA.* Which story is more tragic—the younger son who loses everything and ends up in a pigpen but experiences AHA, or the older son who lives at home with the father and follows all the rules but never experiences AHA?

In fact, his speech reveals that he is disappointed in his father. His words reveal disgust for the extravagant grace shown to his younger brother. He demands an explanation.

The older brother expects what some of the listeners of Jesus's parable were expecting: they want justice for the sinner. They want him to get what he deserves.

## Quandary of the Older Brother

To really understand the point of this parable, you have to look back at the beginning of Luke 15.

> Now the tax collectors and sinners were all gathering around to hear Jesus. But the Pharisees and the teachers of the law muttered, "This man welcomes sinners and eats with them."

Half of the audience for Jesus's parable were the sinners and tax collectors. Spiritually speaking, they were the younger brothers, far from the Father living in the Distant Country. But the Pharisees and teachers of the Law were the older brothers.

They spent their days steeped in study and clergy work. And here they were looking down on Jesus for spending time with the younger brother.

So Jesus used the older brother in the parable to speak to them. He knew that the challenge of being an older brother was that you almost never saw yourself as the older brother. He created a character that had done everything right, a son who had been faithful and worked hard for the father's benefit. This is how many of the Pharisees would have undoubtedly seen themselves. Spiritually speaking, these men literally worked in the Father's house—at the temple—but their hearts were far from Him.

Their understanding of God was flawed. They saw Him as harsh and unforgiving—as a cosmic cop, patrolling the universe, waiting for folks to mess up so He can bust them and hand out an eternal verdict.

Jesus said no, this is our Father: loving, compassionate, caring, beyond our social expectations, willing to search and wait and celebrate and heal the broken. Jesus turned religion on its head, breaking down its exclusive, legalistic barriers and replacing them with welcoming relationship. Jesus painted the Father's portrait with grace, mercy, and nearly unfathomable love.

This is our Father. What kind of son or daughter will we each be?

## *My AHA*

Who are you in the story of the Prodigal Son? Write yourself
in—as you truly are, and then as God truly wants you to be.

_____

_____

_____

_____

_____

_____

_____

_____

# DAY 38

## *You May Be an Older Brother If ...*

*Let us then approach God's throne of grace with*
*confidence, so that we may receive mercy and*
*find grace to help us in our time of need.*
Hebrews 4:16

My brother-in-law is a police officer. Anyone related to a policeman knows that his or her work stories trump everyone else's. My story about discovering the original Greek word for *poop*† is never going to beat his story about rappelling down from a helicopter to incinerate illegally planted marijuana fields.

I remember one time he told me about some different accident scenes that he had come upon, including some with

---

† The word is *skubala*, by the way, used in Philippians 3:8.

pretty serious injuries. I said, "Well, they must be relieved when you show up on the scene. People must feel a lot better when they see you pull up."

He said, "Not really. A lot of times they're pretty nervous, because when I come on the scene, I'm there to investigate. I'm there to assign blame." He paused for a moment before adding, "But they're always glad to see the paramedics. See, the paramedics come in, and their job is to free those who are trapped, bandage those who have been wounded, and help those who are hurting."

The Pharisees listening to Jesus learned what we often forget: faithful followers of Christ aren't on earth to assign blame; we're here to free the trapped, bandage the wounded, help the hurting, and celebrate homecomings.

## The Other Prodigal

The older son was indignant after seeing his father's actions. This older brother may have worked hard and faithfully tended the fields, but he was lost in his father's house.

There was no awakening.

There was no honesty.

There was no action.

The truth is, he, too, was a prodigal son. He, too, had a heart that was far from the father. He, too, was lost, but he didn't see it. Tim Keller put it this way: "So we have two sons, one 'bad' by conventional standards and one 'good,' yet both are alienated from the father."[1]

You may never have been to a Distant Country. You may have an impressive religious résumé. You may have followed all the rules. You may have read this entire book thinking of all the people you know in the Distant Country who really need to hear it. But I wonder if you are the one Jesus has been talking to all along.

Since older brothers have such a difficult time seeing themselves as people in need of AHA—I know, I've been there—I want to give you a few signs to watch for. You may be an older brother if you are ...

## Critical of others' sins

Older brothers often focus on the flaws of others. They're unwilling to recognize any repentance in prodigals, because they can't see past the mistakes. So a person tries to make a truthful turnaround after living a life full of lies, and instead of being encouraging and supportive, an older brother will keep bringing up the lies he or she has told before.

Older brothers often have a hard time celebrating when AHA happens. When someone comes home from the Distant Country repentant and broken and wanting to do things differently, the older brother will cross his arms instead of opening them. He might say, "Let's give it some time," or "Well, you're going to need to make some things right," or maybe, "Well, you need to get your act together."

Well, nobody asked you. This isn't your house. It's the *Father's* house. It's not for you to decide who gets to come home to be called sons and daughters.

When there is a refusal to celebrate, it shows that we have missed the point. We've missed God's grace in our own lives.

If we knew what we had been saved from, if we were aware of our lostness, if we could clearly see our sin—we would never be that way. We would be the first ones to celebrate. The Father would run, and we would run right behind Him, because we know what He's done for us. When I live with an awareness of what He's done for me—*oh man!*—my arms are wide open. But when we miss it, arms get crossed.

## Confident in your goodness

Older-brother syndrome focuses on your own goodness instead of the Father's grace. The older brother basically said,

"Look what I deserve. I've been good. I've followed the rules. I've done what you've asked me to. I deserve your blessing. I've earned it."

This kind of claim made no mention of the father's provision in his life—even though the older brother had lived a life fully dependent on the father. But he was unwilling to acknowledge the father's generosity. Instead, he focused on what he didn't get. He complained that he had never even received a small goat to have a party with his friends. How long had the older brother felt this way? Probably ever since his father first gave the younger son half the inheritance.

The problem with confidence in our own goodness is that we believe we're going to earn something from the Father. But the Father's house is not a house of merit; it is a house of mercy.

While the older brother claims, "I've never disobeyed"; the younger brother says, "I am not worthy." One brother appeals to his own merit; the other comes asking for mercy. One brother sulks in frustration; the other celebrates in joy. Until you go from "I've never disobeyed" to "I am not worthy," you will not have AHA.

# Why Jesus Is So Hard on the Older Brothers

Look, I know this sounds harsh.

You may be reading this and thinking, *If Jesus is so merciful, why is He so tough on the Pharisees?* That's a fair question.

Here's what I think: Jesus knew that most people would base what they thought about God, and what they thought God was like, on how the Pharisees and teachers of the Law lived and behaved. It's even true today. The way employees interact with us sways what we think of the entire company. I mean, if you walk into a department store with your family and encounter a sales representative who is pushy in his pitch and uses foul language in front of your kids, you're not going to be happy. While you may take issue with him personally, what are you going to say? "I'd like to speak to the manager, please."

Jesus knew—and knows—there are a lot of older brothers totally misrepresenting the heart of God. None of us will ever be perfect, but those filled with thankfulness for love and life they know they don't deserve will be marked with grace, mercy, and love. And they will draw others to the Father rather than send them toward the Distant Country.

## My AHA

List and confess any tendencies of older-brother syndrome in your life.

_____

_____

_____

_____

_____

_____

_____

_____

# DAY 39

## *All about the Father*

*Praise be to the God and Father of our Lord Jesus Christ,
who has blessed us in the heavenly realms with every
spiritual blessing in Christ. For he chose us in him before the
creation of the world to be holy and blameless in his sight.
In love he predestined us for adoption to sonship through
Jesus Christ, in accordance with his pleasure and will.*

Ephesians 1:3–5

A friend of mine told me about an elderly man he knew who could no longer take care of himself and whose family made the difficult decision for him to live in a nursing home. Every Sunday afternoon the man's daughter and her husband and children would go visit him. Every Sunday this elderly man would wait for his daughter and her family to come visit. He looked forward to it all week and was always out waiting for them. As the years passed, his mind grew weaker, and he soon had a hard time remembering his children's names. He would sometimes have a hard time getting back to his room.

But no matter what happened, on Sunday afternoon, he was always there waiting for his daughter and her family.

One day the daughter asked her father, "Daddy, do you know what day of the week it is?" He couldn't tell her what day of the week it was. So she said to him, "Well, Daddy, how did you know to wait for us today?"

The father replied, "Oh, honey, I wait for you every day."

God is a loving Father who longs for His children to come home. On the day you finally come home, you will find Him waiting for you. You might wonder, *How did He know to wait for me on this day? How did He know I was coming today?*

He has been waiting for you every day.

## Unexpected

As we've seen, the story of the Prodigal Son is really about the Father. And AHA is about us responding, returning, and relating to Him. Jesus's parable is an invitation and an explanation of God as our Father.

It's a vivid reminder that our Father seeks out both kinds of sons and that He offers love and grace to both.

You see, both sons were in the wrong, and it was really both of their responsibilities to seek out the father. But the father didn't wait. He wasn't proud and indignant about being disrespected. He ran to his younger son, and he sought his older son in the fields.

What does this tell us about God? God longs for a relationship with His children.

But a relationship isn't what the sons deserved. The father had every right to come down hard on both of his sons. Those listening to this parable would have agreed that the father was well within his rights to deal out justice and punishment to both sons.

But after the younger son's insulting choices and reckless living, the father embraced him with kisses and hugs. And after the older brother's harsh words and disrespect, the father lovingly explained himself. The patriarch would never have had to explain himself in ancient times. Households were not democracies; they were dictatorships. Yet the father answered the older brother's anger with gentle patience and grace.

We expect God to be an angry Father who demands justice, but through Jesus, He gives us love and grace when we don't deserve it. We want to hide our sin and our shortcomings, but our Father wants to run and silence our explanations with joyous kisses. We rely on our rules and count our accomplishments, but God invites us to celebrate and savor His loving favor that we can't possibly earn.

Ultimately, the story in Luke 15 isn't about two sons who disobey. It is about a Father who loves His children unconditionally and extravagantly.

Ultimately, AHA is an ongoing process. It is continually awakening to the Holy Spirit's voice, responding openly and honestly to God, and taking action toward and out of our Father's love. AHA is relating to our heavenly Father. It is living with our eyes and hearts open to Him. It's receiving and giving and experiencing and being shaped by our Father's transformative love.

This is what God our Father is waiting for. This is only the beginning of what He offers in His open arms.

## My AHA

Let it all go in the Father's embrace.

*Father, here I am with no pretense. I want and I need You. Everything else is Yours. I bring You …*

# DAY 40

## *More to the Story*

*Taste and see that the LORD is good; blessed
is the one who takes refuge in him.*

Psalm 34:8

One of my favorite Old Testament stories is found in the book of 2 Kings, where the king of Aram, an enemy of Israel, sent a great army to surround one of Israel's cities and destroy God's prophet Elisha.

Elisha was with his servant when the enemy attacked, and the two of them were surrounded. The servant was terrified and cried out to Elisha. My guess is that he cried out with a sense of sheer panic, saying to Elisha, "Master! What are we going to do?"

Elisha responded with a remarkable statement. He said, "Don't be afraid. Those who are with us are more than those who are with them" (2 Kings 6:16).

Elisha's servant looked around, but there was no one with them! They were all alone. It was the two of them against an army. Then Elisha prayed a simple prayer for his servant. He prayed: "God, open his eyes so that he may see."

Then we're told, "The LORD opened the servant's eyes, and he looked and saw the hills full of horses and chariots of fire all around Elisha" (v. 17). His eyes were opened and—AHA—he suddenly realized that heavenly forces protected them and there had been nothing to fear in the first place.

# More to Your Story

There was more to the story. There is always more to the story. There is more to your story. Wherever you are, you are not too far to reach God. Whoever you are in the story of the Prodigal Son—the prodigal, the father, or the older brother—you are not beyond hope for healing and restoration. God is at work all around you.

Take heart that the God of the possible is at work all around you in unseen ways. When you feel alone, may our Father open your heart to His presence. When you see nothing but darkness, may He open your eyes to a glimpse of His ability. When the Distant Country beckons, may He overwhelm you with contentment and joy. And when fear or despair grip your soul, may He fill you with the rest and peace of one protected by His heavenly hand. May you be able to open your eyes and see.

Elisha's prayer for his servant is my prayer for you today.

*God, open her eyes and let her see that though he walked out on her, You will never leave her, and she is not alone.*

*God, open his eyes so he can see a wife who is cold and hard only because she doesn't feel safe enough to be vulnerable with him.*

*God, open his eyes that he may see he is living his life to impress others and glorify himself, which leads only to emptiness.*

*God, open her eyes and let her see that a beautifully decorated and well-kept house has become more important to her than a joyful and peaceful home.*

*God, open her eyes so she can see that You are able to work for good, even out of the darkest and most painful circumstances.*

*God, open his eyes and let him see that You have plans and a purpose for his life—plans for good.*

*God, open her eyes and let her see that You created her uniquely, specially, a one-of-a-kind masterpiece filled with Your beauty.*

*God, open her eyes and let her see that the material wealth and possessions of this world will never satisfy.*

*God, open his eyes and let him see the single mom who lives next door with a young son who doesn't know how to throw a football.*

*God, open our eyes and let us see the hungry and the hurting living just a few miles down the road.*

*God, open our eyes and let us see that neither death nor life, neither angels nor demons, neither the present nor the future, nor any powers, neither height nor depth, nor anything else in all creation will be able to separate us or our prodigals from the love of God that is in Christ Jesus our Lord.*

*God, open our eyes and let us see the pride that has blinded us, the sin that has hardened us, and the lies that have deceived us.*

*Lord, we pray for AHA. Awaken us.*

## My AHA

*God, open my eyes and let me see …*

_____

_____

_____

_____

# NOTES

## Day 7—Erasing Famines

1. Adapted from John Ortberg, "Don't Waste a Crisis," *Leadership Journal, Christianity Today*, Winter 2011, www.christianity today.com/le/2011/winter/dontwastecrisis.html?start=5.

## Day 8—Getting What We Deserve

1. Ruth Schenk, "'AHA Experience' Offers Hope for the Prodigal," *The Southeast Outlook*, March 13, 2014, www.southeastoutlook.org/news/top_stories/article_ 687e4a4c-a9f8-11e3-9787-001a4bcf6878.html.

## Day 9—Redeeming the Pain

1. Gerald L. Sittser, *A Grace Disguised: How the Soul Grows Through Loss* (Grand Rapids, MI: Zondervan, 2009), 17–18.

## Day 10—Escaping the Country of the Blind

1. H. G. Wells, "The Country of the Blind," *The Literature Network*, www.online-literature.com/wellshg/3/.

## Day 12—In Plain Sight

1. Michael Martinez, "Life on the Lam: Bulger, Girlfriend Enjoyed Ocean Breezes, Fine Dining," CNN Justice, June 25, 2011, www.cnn.com/2011/CRIME/06/24/california .bulger.profile/index.html.

## Day 15—Honest with Myself

1. "Lance Armstrong's Confession," Oprah's Next Chapter, Oprah Winfrey Network, January 17, 2013, www.youtube .com/watch?v=N_0PSZ59Aws.
2. Susan Wise Bauer, *The Art of the Public Grovel: Sexual Sin and Public Confession in America* (Princeton: Princeton University Press, 2008), 2.

## Day 16—Honesty That Brings Healing

1. Jason Straziuso, "Rwanda Genocide: Man and Victim Now Friends," Associated Press, April 6, 2014, bigstory.ap.org /article/rwanda-genocide-man-and-victim-now-friends.
2. C. R. Snyder, *Coping with Stress: Effective People and Processes* (New York: Oxford University Press, 2001), 205, 200.

## Day 18—One Step at a Time

1. "Bernie Madoff's Apology," *The Daily Beast*, June 29, 2009, www.thedailybeast.com/articles/2009/06/29/bernie -madoffs-apology.html.

2. Jim Collins, "The Secret Life of the CEO: Is the Economy Just Built to Flip?" *Fast Company*, October 2002, www.jimcollins .com/article_topics/articles/the-secret-life.html.

## Day 21—Blame Game

1. "Top 10 Outrageous Legal Battles: So Sue Me, A 'Class' Action," *Time*, content.time.com/time/specials/packages /article/0,28804,1899500_1899502_1914603,00.html.

2. Ashley Jennings, "Idaho Inmates Sue Beer, Wine Companies for $1B," *ABC News*, January 3, 2013, http:// abcnews.go.com/blogs/headlines/2013/01/idaho-inmates -sue-beer-wine-companies-for-1b/.

## Day 28—Change or Die

1. Alan Deutschman, "Change or Die," *Fast Company*, May 1, 2005, www.fastcompany.com/52717/change-or-die.

2. "How to Manage Your Stress," *USA Today*, March 7, 2001, http://usatoday30.usatoday.com/news/health/2001-03-07 -stress-tips.htm.

## Day 29—Changing Your Story

1. Lulu Miller, "Editing Your Life's Stories Can Create Happier Endings," NPR, January 1, 2014, www.npr.org/blogs/health/2014/01/01/258674011/editing-your-lifes-stories-can-create-happier-endings.
2. Gareth Cook, "How to Improve Your Life with 'Story Editing,'" *Scientific American*, September 13, 2011, www.scientificamerican.com/article/how-to-improve-your-life-with-story-editing/.

## Day 34—Killing Time

1. Guido of Monte Rochen, *Handbook for Curates: A Late Medieval Manual on Pastoral Ministry*, (Washington, DC: The Catholic University of America Press, 2011), 191.
2. "Procrastination: Readers' Tales of Epic Time-Wasting," August 29, 2012, *BBC News Magazine*, www.bbc.com/news/magazine-19396204.

## Day 38—You May Be an Older Brother If ...

1. Timothy Keller, *The Prodigal God: Recovering the Heart of the Christian Faith*, (New York: Penguin, 2008), 34.

# light up your life

We've all had an "aha!" moment in our lives, an insight that changes everything. With everyday examples and trademark testimonies, Kyle Idleman, bestselling author of *Not a Fan,* draws on Scripture to reveal how three key elements—awakening, honesty, and action—can produce the same kind of "aha!" in our spiritual lives.

kyleidleman.com